Praise

Lead, Motivate, Engage: INSPIRE Your Team to Win at Work

This book offers insights, practical tips, and tools that I can use with my team and leaders I consult with to inspire them to help their teams win. I enjoyed the depth of information the book offers as it helps you really understand the concepts and provides real world examples that you can draw from to apply this to your work everyday. I found the self assessments valuable to identify where I am and where I need to focus on to be successful. This is a great read and definitely a book I will continue to pick up and refer to.

Julio Carmenate
Manager, Organization Development, Warner Brothers

What an exceptional read! With Employee Engagement being at a focal point in business, this book delivers all the right tools, theoretical perspectives, and resources to help excel in this space. The recommended strategies and assessments are golden additions to any manager's toolkit. This book speaks to you in everyday language but delivers a very strong message deeply rooted in and supported by years of research. This is an excellent resource I would recommend to any employee and academician.

Ani Ziyalyan
Director, Program Management and
Transformation, Legal and Compliance, CBRE.

Both epically practical and grounded in foundational leadership theory, *Lead, Motivate, Engage* has provided me with key insights to immediately implement into my talent management practices.

Christine Murphy Hernandez
SVP, Talent Management & Organizational Development,
TMNA Services

Leading, motivating, and engaging employees are some of the most difficult things to accomplish. As a practitioner, it is crucial to have as much knowledge as possible to be able to help clients. Drs. Hilliard and Lopez do an amazing job of providing useful tips and tools that span across the early times of scholarly research to the most recent practitioner tactics. The authors understand that the best way to serve a client is by integrating and translating theories in ways that they can apply them. If you are a manager, leader, or practitioner and looking to improve your toolkit to INSPIRE your team to win – look no further!

Abraham M. Gutsioglou
CEO, Think Differently LLC

Many books explain "What" is engagement and "Why" it is important. But this valuable book tells you "How" to engage your employees. The book contains many practical tools to help you with this important task. In addition the case examples provide illustrations of how engagement practices have been applied. I highly recommend this book for managers who want to have engaged and high performing employees.

Dr. Petti Van Rekom
Professor of Performance Improvement Leadership

LEAD, MOTIVATE, ENGAGE

How to INSPIRE Your Team to Win at Work

PEARL HILLIARD
EDD

DENISE LOPEZ
PHD

People Performance Publishing
Pearl Hilliard
Patricia "Denise" Lopez
https://leadmotivateengage.com/
info@leadmotivateengage.com

ISBN: 9781793814111

Dedication

To leaders who want to feel excited about
going to work and inspiring their team members

*"The greatest leader is not necessarily the one
who does the greatest things. He is the one
that gets the people to do the greatest things."*
–Ronald Reagan

Table of Contents

List of Tools

Please note: These tools are available online, in Word format, so you can customize for your own use. See the URL on the "Invitation" page – towards the end of the book.

Preface

Have you looked up at the sky and marveled at flocks of birds flying overhead in a "V" formation? These migrations happen for various reasons: birds fly between their breeding and non-breeding "homes," they follow food sources and/or water sources, they fly to warmer climates in the winter, etc. We usually notice the geese and ducks (perhaps because of their noisy calls!), but many other species also fly in a V. They fly this way so that all the birds (except the lead bird) fly in the "upwash" – the rising air – of the bird in front of them. Recent research has shown that each bird flies in partnership with the bird in front of them, flying a specific distance behind the bird and at a specific angle.[1] Their wing beats are precisely timed with the bird in front, so the air updraft is maximized, and thus energy expended is minimized. If the bird in front of them changes its wing beat, then the one behind changes too, and the one behind that, etc. What an amazing feat of optimization and synchronicity!

We really liked the symbolism of a flock of birds (which is why we have that on our cover). The bird at the front of the "V" formation does the hardest job, and when he/she is tired, a different bird takes over – that's the kind of team work we're advocating for engaged teams – the manager doesn't necessarily take the lead all the time. We also like the concept of cooperation between the birds – how they are sensitive to the bird in front of them, so that they modify their actions, which results in less effort and better results. Engaged teams do this too, with the members knowing they are all in it together and have each other's backs. Success happens when team members support each other in their joint efforts to achieve the goals of the organization. Teamwork, shared leadership, optimization and synchronicity are key.

The authors, Dr. Pearl Hilliard and Dr. Denise Lopez, met quite a few years ago in a professional capacity. They bonded over their joint passion for employee engagement, team building and authentic leadership. They examined their own experiences with various managers, as well as the experiences of their clients. These discussions evolved into ideas for helping leaders become more successful, and so the notion of this book was born.

Pearl always envied the people who knew at age 6, 16 or 21 what they wanted to be … an architect, lawyer, teacher, doctor, engineer, etc. She took a winding road, trying out different careers, and it was only when she "fell" into the training and development field that she found out what she loved to do. That discovery made a huge difference to her happiness and engagement at work. Now, she is energized and fulfilled. She remembers those other jobs and how disengaged she was – how it was such a drag to go to work every day. This experience led her to focus on strengths development, employee engagement and what it takes for teams to be successful. (She also realizes that there were some actions she could have taken in those previous positions that would have resulted in more engagement and less dissatisfaction – if only she had this book to read back then!)

Denise also took a winding road in her education and career to find what truly engaged her and utilized her passions and strengths. As she sought to define herself, she experimented with all types of college majors from biology to computer science and ultimately to psychology and, later, industrial-organizational psychology. Today she finds fulfillment in a career that spans teaching, research, leadership coaching and organizational consulting. All of these are challenging and provide meaning to her life. Denise has no regrets that she took a winding professional road because she has discovered that every person's journey of personal and professional discovery runs parallel to the one all leaders need to experience in order to be effective and engaging. That is, in order to influence and engage others, the leader needs to take a deep look at what engages him- or herself. Moreover, the only way to get better is to listen and learn from others from all levels and all walks of life, try new behaviors, and keep adapting.

In your experience as a leader, you have probably managed some employees and teams who are fully engaged and a delight to work with. On the other hand, you've probably led other employees who didn't get excited about anything! As a manager, what can you do about this latter group? Both authors have managed these two kinds of employees and we want to share our knowledge and experience with you.

The purpose of this book is to provide tools and tips to help you lead, motivate and engage your employees. We've taken a scholar-practitioner approach in preparing this book. We analyzed the various experiences of our clients. We reviewed multiple theories and frameworks from the fields of psychology, work motivation and leadership, and combed through reams of academic, consulting and industry research. Then we sought to translate these experiences, theories and findings into practical recommendations that leaders can use in the workplace.

You will notice that we utilize a variety of resources, from those describing classic foundational theories dating from the 1960's to the

1990's, to new and contemporary research as recent as 2018-2019 from academic and consulting sources. We believe in describing and applying the best ideas no matter when these were originated, so long as they remain relevant to leaders and organizations today. At the same time, we have intentionally searched for material with a focus on the Millennial demographic.

The definitions of a "leader" and "manager" are different. A leader is an influencer, an engager and a visionary who is focused on the future. This individual may or may not have a formal leadership title. A manager has positional authority to plan, organize, control and direct employees to achieve departmental goals. The manager often focuses on the here and now – the required results – and isn't necessarily innovative or personally influential. In this book, we are taking the liberty of using the words interchangeably as we believe that the current engaging manager is also a leader.

At each level of the organization, there are roles and responsibilities that support a successful and high-engagement culture. Our principal focus is on the manager. What can the manager do to effectively engage employees? While most existing research has focused on organizational and task conditions and leadership characteristics that are correlated with employee engagement, there is not as much research focused on what individual managers can specifically do at the behavioral level to engage their people.

Even though this book is written for managers, it takes the perspective of employees too. (After all, managers are employees as well.) Which actions and strategies encourage your own engagement at work? In addition, we take a 50,000-foot view of the organization and its responsibilities in supporting the engagement of employees and leaders, and we list the best practices for the organization.

Even though you, as a leader, may not have much control over the organization's processes, maybe there are some areas where you can influence the organization to elevate its systems in order to promote employee engagement and team success.

We have organized our recommendations on leading, motivating and engaging people around seven components with the INSPIRE acronym (ignite, nurture – career development, use of strengths, effective performance management, inclusion, relationships at work, and empowerment). We selected "Nurture" for the career development component, not only because there is no "C" in INSPIRE (!!) but also because it denotes what effective leaders do with their team members. While there are many leadership frameworks around, we believe our model is unique because it leverages multiple perspectives around engagement, leadership, positive psychology, empowerment, diversity and inclusion using a scholar-practitioner model. We hope this is something that managers will find useful in expanding their understanding and guiding their actions around employee engagement.

You'll also notice that we have included a lot of research. This is to give credibility to our model and the suggestions in this book. The "nerds" amongst you will enjoy this. Those of you who aren't interested in the research can skip these sections and dive right into the practicalities …

Here's a quick overview of each chapter:

1. **Ignite** your team through positive communication and meaningful work: Ideas for how leaders can motivate and energize their teams through the creation of an inspiring vision, appreciative communication and the provision of

work that is meaningful and aligned both with the organization's mission and the employee's values.

2. **Nurture** your people: Suggestions for enhancing retention and engagement by championing the personal growth and career development of your team members. The three roles of coach/facilitator, career driver and the organizational support system are addressed.

3. Leverage employee **Strengths**: Are you optimizing the strengths of your employees and your team? It's a win-win situation when your direct report's strengths are amplified and used to achieve the individual's, department's and organization's goals.

4. Use **Performance Management** to engage employees: Effective and collaborative goal setting is at the heart of a successful team. Foster a culture of universal accountability and focus on future-based, developmental coaching.

5. Be **Inclusive**: Do your team members feel involved, valued and fully integrated into the organization? To create trusting relationships with your employees, it is imperative that you are fair, respectful and genuine. Four key, inclusive leadership behaviors are discussed.

6. **Relate** with authenticity and emotional Intelligence: Are you authentic and do you have strong, positive relationships with your employees? This chapter covers the steps in effective relationship management, the components of emotional intelligence and criteria for authentic leadership.

7. **Empower**: How do you ensure that your team members are ready, willing and able to be empowered? This chapter describes three important empowering manager behaviors and explains how to align empowerment strategies with cultural values and the distinctive work context.

How to Use This Book

All seven chapters are stand-alone chapters, and you can delve into the area that most interests you or where you feel you can make the most impact immediately. We suggest that you begin by perusing the introduction, which addresses mindset. Then take the INSPIRE Engagement Behavior Survey (Leader Self-Assessment) – Appendix A, which is towards the end of the book. This is a self-assessment of the extent to which you engage in various leadership behaviors that motivate and engage your team members.

We have an INSPIRE Engagement Scale (for Team Members) – Appendix B. This is a short team member engagement scale with items tailored to our own definition of employee engagement. Some of the items are inspired by other scales such as the Utrecht Work Engagement Scale.[2]

There is also an INSPIRE Engagement Behavior Survey (Team Member Assessment of Manager) – Appendix C. The INSPIRE Engagement Scale (Appendix B), along with the Team Member Assessment of Manager Behaviors (Appendix C), can be administered to your team to determine its current level of engagement, as well as its perceptions of your behaviors as a leader. This way, you will know your areas of strength and areas of opportunity. (We recommend that someone from a different department administer and compile the results for you, so the responses are anonymous to you.) Once you have implemented some of the recommended actions in this book, you can administer these assessments again to see the changes that have occurred. The results may also point you to the next component where you could make the most impact.

We are currently in the process of validating these assessments to keep improving the quality of the instruments. We would love to collaborate with you to continue collecting anonymous employee data for this validation project – see our "Invitation" towards the end of the book.

Each chapter includes:

- **Reflections/Exercises** – giving you the opportunity to consider your own experiences.
- **Survey questions** – from the INSPIRE Engagement Behavior Survey (Leader Self-Assessment) – Appendix A. The questions pertain to the topic of the chapter.
- **Recommendations for Leaders** – how you can enhance the engagement of your team members.
- **Recommendations for Employees** – suggestions for individuals on how they can increase their own engagement (this includes you!).
- **Organizational Best Practices** – you'll be able to see what the "best-in-class" organizations do (even though you don't necessarily have control over these structures/procedures)
- **Case examples** – show how some individuals / organizations are helping their teams to win at work.
- **Deeper dives** – where we go into greater detail, perhaps reviewing academic research. These dives will probably be appreciated by the nerds amongst us! These sections are shaded

a light grey, so it's easy for you to skip over them (if the deeper dive isn't of that much interest to you), and you can jump right into the core material.

- **Takeaways** – the most pertinent learnings, at the end of each chapter.
- **Tools – Checklists / Appendices** – useful resources which you can use/apply right away.
- **The endnotes** – references used in each chapter – are towards the end of the book in the "Endnotes" chapter.

Throughout the book, when we are writing about the individual employee (instead of employees in general) we will alternate the use of "he" and "she" pronouns.

We know that some of you want to get started right away! Our aim is for this book to be a toolkit that you can delve into whenever the need arises. Please go to the "Invitation" page (towards the end of the book) for the URL where you will find all the tools online, in Word format. You can easily customize these forms and checklists to fit your situation.

Thank you for reading our book. Feel free to provide feedback, ideas and suggestions to us at info@leadmotivateengage.com.

Introduction

Leadership and the Engagement Mindset

. . . .

"There are only three measurements that tell you nearly everything you need to know about your organization's overall performance: employee engagement, customer satisfaction, and cash flow ... It goes without saying that no company, small or large, can win over the long run without energized employees who believe in the mission and understand how to achieve it."
– Jack Welch, former CEO of GE

. . . .

In the last few decades, two of the most important concepts that have continued to capture the attention of leaders and management consultants are "leadership" and "employee engagement." Every year, companies spend millions of dollars on leadership development programs, coaching and training, as well as employee engagement surveys and initiatives.

As mentioned in our preface, the goal of our book is to provide leaders and managers with useful insights and tools to lead, motivate and engage teams successfully. Let's start by defining some key terms and by highlighting the importance of having the appropriate engagement mindset to enact the seven components of our INSPIRE model.

Leadership, Motivation and Employee Engagement Defined

There are so many perspectives on leadership. Academics have tried to define it in terms of leadership traits, behaviors, relationships with others, charisma, transformational capabilities, authenticity, ethical and servant leadership, etc. In a nutshell though, leadership is the act of inspiring and mobilizing people towards a desired future.

Motivation refers to the reason(s) that influence whether people decide to pursue a certain course of action, how much effort they exert, and how long they sustain their efforts. These reasons could be internal (such as personal values and interest) or external (rewards or punishment). Knowing how to motivate others and mobilize them to pursue a shared team or organizational objective is a core aspect of being a leader.

In recent years, the study of human motivation has focused on the concept of engagement. Researchers and consultants have begun to demonstrate how high employee engagement predicts individual and organizational performance. One challenge to applying this in the workplace is that the concept of engagement has been confused with other terms, especially job satisfaction.

Job satisfaction refers to employee attitudes about their job. It typically encompasses how employees think and feel about specific job aspects such as the work conditions, roles and responsibilities, the supervisor, and their pay and benefits.

In contrast, we define employee engagement as a state characterized by enthusiasm, inspiration, and positive energy, psychological empowerment, and the sense of being fully connected with one's work and other people. Noted researchers of engagement similarly define engagement as a positive, fulfilling, work-related state of mind that is characterized by vigor, dedication and absorption.[1] Taking this even further, William Kahn – the originator of the term work engagement – defines an engaged individual as one who is fully present (physically, cognitively and emotionally) in his or her work, because the work itself allows the full expression of the person's "preferred self."[2]

Thus, being engaged is an active, involved state while being satisfied with one's job tends to be a more passive condition dependent on the fulfillment of the basic requirements of the job. We can imagine satisfied employees not complaining about what they are doing on the job, how they are being managed or how they are being rewarded. However satisfied employees will not necessarily be as excited or willing to go the extra mile to be productive, innovative and supportive of the organization's mission and vision as engaged employees would be.

It is important for leaders, employees and consultants to note how engagement (or any other concept for that matter) is being defined since definitions drive how we measure and track important outcomes in organizations. There is considerable research going on in terms of leader assessment and employee- engagement surveys. Knowing whether or not, and how, leader characteristics and behaviors are related with employee engagement is the first step to identifying and designing interventions to enhance engagement in organizations. As a general tip to our readers: know what outcomes you desire and carefully consider how these are being measured. (Refer to Appendix B for our Inspire Engagement Scale for Team Members, which is based on our definition of engagement described above. We also provide a leader self-assessment of engagement behaviors – Appendix A, as well as a corresponding team member assessment of the leader's engagement behaviors – Appendix C).

Why does employee engagement matter to leaders?

Several domestic and global organizations from leading consulting firms like Gallup, The Hay Group, Watson Wyatt, and CEB (now Gartner) regularly collect data and report on the state of employee engagement across industries, with results suggesting that a large proportion of the workforce (e.g., up to 2/3 of employees) are not engaged at work. Large multinational companies conduct their own annual surveys, with many indicating that a large percentage of their employees (40% or more) are not very engaged either. Low employee engagement numbers fuel a sense of urgency within managers and organizations to pay attention to employee engagement because how employees think and feel has a significant impact on the work environment and business outcomes. As mentioned earlier though, it is important to pay attention to how employee engagement is measured and reported. Depending on the type of questions and response scales that are used, engagement numbers may vary greatly.

Nevertheless, research has shown that employee engagement is positively related to commitment, retention, job performance, citizenship behaviors (or proactive work), creativity and innovation. Companies with highly engaged employees have 2.5 times higher revenue growth than their counterparts, and 40% less turnover of highly skilled staff.[3] Disengagement has been connected with work slowdowns and loafing, higher rates of absenteeism, suboptimal work and even theft rates.

Here's some more convincing data: In 2018, The Drucker Institute released its second annual ranking of America's largest publicly traded companies.[4] The rating of these 250 companies is for their overall effectiveness. It is interesting to note that the top 50 companies scored 66.6% for "employee engagement and development overall," whereas the companies that ranked 51 to 250 scored only 46% in this area. There were many other factors that went in to the overall ranking measurement, but a 20% difference in engagement and development is telling – if your organization wants to be at the top, it needs to ensure that its employees are motivated, engaged and developed. This book will help you do that.

The Engagement Mindset

Before we continue discussing the seven components of our INSPIRE engagement model, we want to emphasize the importance of the manager's engagement mindset as the foundation for success. By engagement mindset, we refer to the manager's basic assumptions and philosophy about leading people.

It is our belief that leadership is first and foremost a process of engagement to influence, motivate, organize and empower individuals, teams and organizations towards a desired future. A person cannot lead successfully without engaging others. At the same time, it is not very useful to discuss employee engagement outside the context of leadership and organizational priorities. It is the successful balance of these three (leadership behaviors, organizational priorities, and engagement) that successful leaders must achieve.

A few years ago, research by Deloitte indicated that 86% of business and HR leaders believe they have an inadequate leadership pipeline. At the same time, 79% of these leaders stated that they have a significant engagement and retention issue, with 75% indicating they have a hard time attracting and recruiting the top people they need. Interestingly, only 17% of these HR and business leaders believed they have a compelling and engaging employment brand.[5] This suggests that HR and business leaders recognize the employee engagement issue in their companies though very few appear to be satisfied with where they are on the matter.

Certainly, organizations can continue investing time and money on various programs that can be done to attract top people to their companies, how to engage them, and so forth. It is our contention that unless managers change how they fundamentally view and interact with their people, they may not be able to create and sustain engagement and performance for the long term. In other words, putting in place engagement and leadership initiatives is well and good, but these initiatives need to incorporate the appropriate mindset among managers about what it means to lead and engage people.

In organizations, we often hear employees being referred to as "human capital" or "human assets." While well-intentioned, these terms fall flat when it comes to trying to inspire and engage people. Why? Because this perspective is akin to thinking of people as resources or things to be managed. Yet, unlike other resources like money, computers or tractors, what makes us "human" is the fact that we think, we feel, we have opinions, we have goals and we have dreams. We strive for growth and choice. We seek to build identities. We want to make our unique mark in this world. Hence, for leaders to truly engage people, they must shift their assumptions about human nature from viewing people as being passive or employable assets to being fully capable and growth-oriented partners in the organization.

Decades ago, Douglas McGregor wrote about the assumptions that managers hold about employees.[6] He called these assumptions "Theory X" and "Theory Y."

What's important to note about these differing assumptions is that they drive management style and behaviors; with enough senior managers sharing the same assumptions about human nature, this could ultimately shape the structure, culture and systems of the organization.

DEEPER DIVE

Theory X and Theory Y[6]

According to McGregor (1960), Theory X managers believe human beings are by nature lazy. They don't like working, and either need to be prodded continuously, threatened by punishment or else enticed by external rewards to work. Theory X managers believe their employees cannot be trusted to accept responsibility and work autonomously, and therefore they need to supervise their employees very closely or else they will slack off. Theory X managers rely on the "carrot and stick" approach to motivation, believing that workers need sufficient reinforcement to get their work done. Put enough Theory X managers into an organization, and you'll end up with a very autocratic, control-oriented culture, with a bureaucratic structure and reward system that is very transactional. Employees are viewed as little more than machines, and the work that is given to them is typically routine and repetitive. You can tell that we are not very fond of this approach because there is essentially no appreciation of employees as people with skills, emotions, goals, and aspirations. McGregor noted that there could be a few instances where Theory X is relevant, for example, low-skilled/blue-collar occupations or mass-production environments where a tight style of management may be appropriate. However, we argue that it is possible to use a different "theory" in blue-collar environments and come out with more engaged and high-performing employees.

The opposite of Theory X is Theory Y. Theory Y managers believe human beings are naturally motivated to learn, grow and take on responsibility. Given the chance, employees will respond positively to more challenging jobs and can manage themselves to meet work goals autonomously. Because of this assumption, Theory Y managers utilize a more participative style of management, consulting with their employees and even allowing them to make decisions about how to structure their work. This type of management theory fits well in today's knowledge economy where employees have more education and skills, and thus seek interesting and challenging jobs with broader scopes of responsibility. Theory Y organizations would thus be expected to have flatter structures with fewer managers because the workers would essentially be managing themselves.

Theory Y comes close to what we consider an appropriate mindset that would support employee engagement in today's organizations.

Essentially, Theory Y challenges managers to treat employees in the way they would want to be treated themselves – as mature, capable individuals. We have seen more and more organizations like Zappos and Google start to adopt this philosophy over the years. However it's been slower to catch on with more organizations than expected because of manager concerns about fully embracing Theory Y. Why? Because at the heart of Theory Y (aka the engagement mindset) is full trust in one's employees. Cynical managers will argue that this theory is a bit too Pollyannaish. Where are the controls? Where is the structure? What if employees cheat? What if they let the manager down? How can the manager ensure that employee behaviors are aligned with the broader organizational goals? How can managers sustain employee performance in the near and long term?

Theory Y might have been ahead of its time in the 1960's, but it seems to be appropriate in today's work environment. However one limitation of Theory Y was that while it provided a positive and humanistic philosophy that many managers could agree with in principle, it was difficult to figure out how to implement it while ensuring that hard business objectives would be achieved.

In this book, we offer a set of seven recommendations on how leaders can put the engagement mindset into concrete action. Each of the seven steps we describe has at its core the assumption that employees are motivated and capable individuals who seek to make meaningful contributions through their work. We predict that as more and more managers take these various steps to lead, motivate and engage their employees, a positive and engaging workplace culture will emerge within the organization.

The engagement mindset as well as the seven components of our INSPIRE model are in line with various new trends of leadership that underscore fundamental shifts in how people view leadership and how people these days want to be led. These new trends recognize the importance of emotional intelligence, shared leadership, positive psychology, strengths and growth mindset, diversity and inclusion, autonomy and empowerment. Based on the engagement mindset, the manager is not the sole driver or controller of what happens in organizations. In fact, it is likely to be a problem if he remains the sole decision-maker for an extended period. Leaders who adopt the engagement mindset need to be ready, willing and able to assume new roles such as mentor, coach, facilitator, liaison and architect. By so doing, they not only engage their employees and contribute to team and organizational success, but they also start to engage themselves and grow as leaders!

Chapter 1

Ignite Your Team through Positive Communication and Meaningful Work

The first step to leading, motivating and engaging employees is to ignite a sense of excitement and inspiration that spurs them to take positive action. We like to use the term "ignite" because it connotes a feeling of energy and arousal. The Merriam-Webster dictionary defines ignite as "to set something on fire" or "to give life or energy to someone or something." Let's start this discussion about "igniting" as a key component of engagement by answering two questions:

1. **What** ignites you at work? (What gets you going? Stimulated? Excited?)
2. **Who** ignites you at work? (Specifically which people, whether leaders, supervisors or team members, ignite you? How do they communicate with you? What do they do that excites and energizes you?)

Refer to Tool 1.1 at the end of this chapter for a useful exercise called "Your Engagement Spark Plugs."

What strikes you about your responses to these questions? We predict that two "spark plugs" that will typically come up have to do with positive and inspiring communication from your leaders and colleagues, and the meaningfulness of your work. And chances are, these will also ignite the members of your team. These two themes are discussed in more detail in the rest of this chapter.

Positive Communication

....

"The art of communication is the language of leadership."
–James Humes

"A leader is a dealer in hope."
–Napoleon

"People will forget what you said and did,
but they will never forget how you made them feel."
–Maya Angelou

....

These are three of our favorite quotations about leadership. The first one calls out the fundamental importance of communication in leading and engaging others while the latter two highlight the impact of positive, inspiring communication on others. Done effectively, positive communication ignites people.

Before reading further, assess your positive communication skills by completing the survey below using the scale:

Never (N), Rarely (R), Sometimes (S), Often (O) and Always (A).

At the bottom of the table, total the number of times you circle each letter. Consider your pattern:

- Which behaviors are you often or always doing? These indicate areas of strength for you.
- Which behaviors are you never or rarely doing? These indicate behaviors that you should try to do more frequently.

Rating	Positive Communication
N R S O A	1. I communicate an inspiring vision for the future.
N R S O A	2. I frequently discuss the importance of the work we do.
N R S O A	3. I am clear about goals and expectations.
N R S O A	4. I listen actively for understanding.
N R S O A	5. I encourage new and creative ideas.
N R S O A	6. I demonstrate appreciation for my team members' contributions.
N R S O A	7. I focus on constructive solutions to individual and team challenges.
N R S O A	8. I express confidence in my team members' abilities.

Research has shown that communication is the number one leadership behavior to engage employees. Interestingly, most managers believe they communicate effectively, but their subordinates often don't agree. As an example, Figure 1 shows the perception gap between how often managers say they recognize employees for good performance and subordinates' perception of the same behavior from their managers.[1]

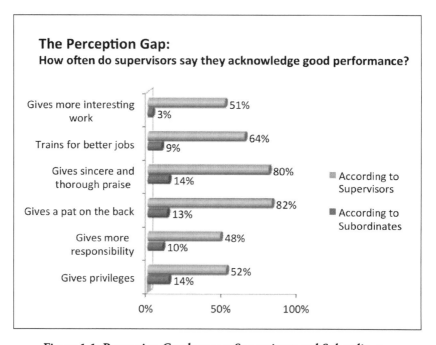

Figure 1.1: Perception Gap between Supervisors and Subordinates

Robinson & Hayday, from the Institute of Employment Studies, asked several organizations in the United Kingdom to identify highly engaging managers, based on recent employee engagement surveys.[2] Once these engaging managers were identified, they conducted interviews and focus groups among the managers' subordinates and superiors. Six of the top behaviors of engaging managers were related to communication. These were:

- communicates a clear strategic vision
- conveys clearly what is expected
- listens, values and involves team
- supports or backs up the team
- shows empathy
- shows active interest in others

The same researchers also asked employees about the most disengaging behaviors of their managers. Four of the top responses were related to communication:

- lacks empathy / not interested in people
- fails to listen and communicate
- does not motivate or inspire
- blames others / does not take responsibility

Another study showed that the five most frequently-mentioned behaviors of engaging leaders are:[3]

- being a clear communicator
- being positive, inspirational and encouraging
- having a vision and clear goals
- being strategic
- having integrity

We believe that for positive communication from leaders to be motivating and engaging, it must have at least three characteristics: inspiration, appreciation and support.

Inspiring Communication

Inspiring communication reaches both the minds and hearts of people. It is meaningful. It provides vision and direction. It is clear and persuasive, provoking ideas and action.

Inspiring communication is very much linked with transformational leadership. In fact, a review of research reported a consistent, positive relationship between transformational leadership and engagement.[4]

Transformational leaders offer an inspiring vision about an extraordinary future state that is personally meaningful to their audience. They don't just talk about correcting mistakes or making incremental improvements; they challenge people's existing assumptions. They purposely present big ideas and invite others to dream with them. They challenge their followers to aspire toward higher goals and greater creativity and innovation.[5] John F. Kennedy, Martin Luther King, Mahatma Gandhi, Barack Obama, Mother Theresa, Elon Musk, Mary Kay Ash and Mary Robinson (7th president of Ireland) serve as excellent and diverse examples of leaders with these transformational qualities. They have used their oral and written communication skills to ignite and engage their followers to higher levels of commitment and performance.

Case Examples – Elon Musk and Jeff Bezos

Two popular contemporary examples of inspirational leaders are Elon Musk (CEO of Tesla and SpaceX) and Jeff Bezos (CEO of Amazon). Both leaders are trailblazers, turning their respective industries on their heads through their revolutionary vision, focus, passion and drive.

Musk imagined electronic cars, high-speed transportation, reusable rockets, mind-computer interfaces and more, and he is making them a reality.

Bezos redefined bookselling, and ultimately the entire retail industry, as well as people's buying behaviors through the Amazon platform. He is known for being obsessed with extremely high standards of customer satisfaction, which he also applies to selecting and hiring his own team members. Interestingly, Bezos uses three questions to evaluate candidates: a) Will you admire this person? b) Will this person raise the level of effectiveness of the group they are joining? c) How might this person be a superstar?[6] Bezos' questions suggest that leaders are not only looking to inspire their team, but also looking for team members who will inspire their leaders and those around them.

An examination of the most inspiring speeches or vision statements show that they include left-brain and right-brain features.[7] As a quick neuroscience review, the right side of the brain is responsible for creativity and imagination i.e. functions such as music composition, painting and storytelling. The left part of the brain, on the other hand, is responsible for logical thinking and functions related to reading, math and rational analysis.

For vision statements and speeches to inspire, they must first appeal to the personal values, interests, imagination and emotions of the audience rather than merely outline issues, goals and action plans. They must paint exciting pictures of the future and strike at the heart of what really matters to employees. Indeed, inspiring leaders are master storytellers who have the ability to convey a message that hits at hearts and minds.[8] They often tell personal stories that reveal their own humanity and make them very accessible to their followers.

It is primarily the right side of the brain that allows leaders to "ignite" the hearts of their followers. It is then the left side that engages followers' minds and ensures that the vision is credible and feasible. We can see elements of both right- and left-brain thinking in the great speeches of Martin Luther King "I have a Dream", Nelson Mandela's "A Dream for which I am Prepared to Die", Winston Churchill's "Never Give In," and Barack Obama's "Yes we can."

One does not have to be a Martin Luther King or Barack Obama to be an inspiring and engaging leader. Managers can apply these same right- and left-brain principles in their everyday communications with individual employees and teams. For example, when talking about what one's team needs to accomplish, managers can emphasize not only specific goals and tasks, but emphasize why these goals matter, and describe how the team will make a difference to people, groups and the community at large. When speaking with individual employees about improvements they need to make at work, rather than highlight deficits and mistakes, managers can design a conversation focusing on opportunities for growth. They can discuss solutions and the personal and organizational benefits that would result from the change. In this way, the discussion can be experienced by employees as being constructive and inspiring.

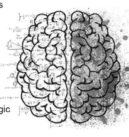

Example Left-Brain Questions

- What are our key strengths as an organization?

- What are our strategic advantages?

- What major issues and obstacles do we face?

- What should be our strategic priorities?

- What outcomes will we accomplish and how will we measure them?

Example Right-Brain Questions

- What is possible for us as an organization?

- How can we reimagine our best possible future?

- What stories or events best describe what we stand for?

- What metaphors, analogies or symbols can capture people's imaginations?

- What kind of colorful and inspirational language can we use to describe our desired future?

To inspire and engage, address the right brain first, then the left brain.

Content of graphic adapted from Whetten & Cameron, 2007, p. 562.[7]

Figure 1.2: Right-Brain and Left-Brain Questions

DEEPER DIVE

Ted Talks are an excellent resource for learning about how to communicate with others in an inspiring way. Here are some of our favorites:[9]

1. **Nancy Duarte: The Secret Structure of Great Talks**
   Nancy Duarte has analyzed the underlying structure of great talks, such as those of Martin Luther King and Steve

Jobs. According to her, inspiring speakers typically paint a picture of an unsatisfactory current state and contrast it with a much more attractive desired future. Inspiring speakers liken themselves or their groups to "regular heroes" who are faced with obstacles and who struggle mightily to reach desired destinations. By so doing, they attain a "new bliss."

2. **Simon Sinek: Start with Why. How Great Leaders Inspire Action**

Simon Sinek describes a three-ringed golden circle of communication, with "why" at the center, surrounded by "how", and then "what". According to him, people typically start with describing the "what" of their goals and jobs, moving to how and why. But the more inspiring leaders start with why, linking their goals and jobs with deeper purpose or meaning, thus engaging the attention and commitment of their audience, before moving to the details of what and how.

3. **Melissa Marshall: Talk Nerdy to Me**

Melissa Marshall is a communication expert who provides great tips to scientists and other technicians trying to present the significance of their work to laypeople. She suggests that scientists easily lose people when they overuse jargon and PowerPoint bullets. Instead, they should emphasize the relevance of their work using everyday terms and engage the audience with the passion they have for their work.

4. Celeste Headlee: Ten Ways to Have a Better Conversation

As a radio host and interviewer, Celeste Headlee declares that the most important twenty-first century skill is the ability to have clear, coherent interpersonal conversations with others. She offers ten tips to having better conversations, including being present in the moment instead of multi-tasking and entering every conversation assuming we have something to learn. She emphasizes the importance of listening versus talking, and that if we listen with the intent to understand, we will most likely be inspired and amazed by others. (This video is relevant not only for positive inspiring communication, but also for relating with emotional intelligence and authenticity, which is discussed in Ch. 6.).

Having read this section and watched at least one of the videos, think of a topic for a future discussion that you want to have with your team or individual employee. For example, it could be about a major change in the department or organization. It could be a discussion about the team's performance with the team leader. Or, it could be a conversation about an employee's career prospects.

Topic:_____

List some strategies (including sample questions and positive conversation starters) that will enhance the likelihood of inspiring your people (include both left-brain and right-brain questions/statements):

1. _____

2. _____

3. _____

4. _____

5. _____

Appreciative Communication

For a leader's communication to engage the team, it must be appreciative.

Appreciative communication approaches people from the standpoint that they are capable, creative and resourceful. Appreciative communication makes recipients feel that they are important – they have skills and experiences that are unique, their views matter, and they are worthy of our attention. Engaging leaders who communicate appreciatively use deep and active listening. They use positive language to build a safe and open environment that encourages people to speak up and leave the conversation feeling validated, recognized, hopeful and inspired.

Neuroscience research has shown that when we appreciate others, we trigger positive emotions like happiness and excitement. Such emotions are likely to result in "generative" (constructive) responses from people rather than defensive reactions.[10]

Barbara Fredrickson describes the "broaden-and-build" effect of positive emotions.[11] Her research has found that feelings such as joy, hope, peace and gratitude serve as resources that not only enhance personal coping and psychological well-being, but also fuel greater physical, cognitive and creative functioning. Positive emotions enhance people's expectations of success, enabling them to set higher goals and become more committed to achieving these goals. As such, positive emotions set people up for "upward spirals" of performance. These positive spirals are often contagious and can create a ripple effect in teams and organizations. As an example, Fredrickson and colleagues conducted research on the effects of loving-kindness meditation workshops and found that these techniques significantly reduced stress levels and increased perceptions of positive emotions and life satisfaction among employees in a large computer company.[12]

Fredrickson proposes using a 3:1 ratio of positive versus negative communication with others. In other words, for every negative or critical thing you convey to team members, make sure you have three positive things to say as well. Though the actual ratio has been debated vigorously by researchers, from a practical perspective we agree that it requires a significant amount of positive feedback and recognition to transform a work environment from one of fear and distrust to a more appreciative and supportive atmosphere. Many of us may have observed, or even experienced, how a single negative comment can have a destructive effect on a person's motivation. Thus, we recommend that managers be inspired by Mark Twain's statement: "I can live for two weeks on a great compliment."

Here are some appreciative statement stems that could be helpful in promoting positive communication and engagement within your team:

Thank you for....
I'm glad you're on our team because...
Congratulations on the great job...
I appreciated how you...
Your contribution in....made a difference in...
I loved your ideas about...

Appreciative communication can also be conveyed by reminding employees of the unique strengths they bring to work and how these strengths make a difference.

Reflection:

Think back to the most appreciative things people have said to you whether at work, home or in another environment. Write these down below. Also think about how these appreciative statements affected your attitudes and behaviors? How did these ignite you?

Now list at least three appreciative statements you can convey to your team this week.

1. _____

2. _____

3. _____

Refer to Chapter 3 for more discussion on using strengths to motivate and engage employees.

Supportive Communication

Supportive communication follows from appreciative communication. We focus on what's going well for the employee, recognizing their strengths, affirming their potential, and reinforcing their successes. We help employees approach issues and challenges using a learning, rather than judgmental perspective. By triggering positive emotions and feelings of safety through supportive behaviors, we allow employees to "broaden and build" solutions that enhance their performance and creativity.

Supportive communication is:[13]

- Descriptive, not evaluative. It promotes information-sharing with others up, down and across the organization, rather than being overly critical and unconstructive. Some examples:
  - *What are the important pieces of data we need to consider? What are the implications of A on B?*
  - *Have we considered the bigger picture?*

- Solution-focused, not blame-seeking. It seeks to reduce defensiveness and open people up to finding novel and useful ways to address problems or challenges. Some examples:
  - *What are different ways we can view and respond to the situation? Let's brainstorm solutions ...*
  - *What can I do to support you?*

- Collaborative, not self-centered. It focuses on building community and having shared goals. Some examples:
  - *How does this situation affect X, Y and Z groups?*
  - *How can you work with X, Y and Z groups to resolve this issue in a way that benefits everyone?*

- Empathetic, not detached. It conveys understanding, caring, and reassurance. Some examples:
  - *Help me understand how you are impacted …*
  - *What concerns do you have that I can address?*

- Confident, not doubting. It communicates your trust in the person's ability to make things happen. Some examples:
  - *What strategies have helped you solve similar problems in the past?*
  - *What strengths and abilities do you bring to this situation?*
  - *Knowing your skills, I have confidence in you …*

Reflection:

Can you think of a current or very recent situation at work where your team (or a specific team member) faced a challenge and needed your support?

As a leader, what can you do to convey your support through words and deeds? List your best ideas.

1. _____

2. _____

3. _____

Additional ideas related to positive communication are provided in Chapter 2 (Nurturing), Chapter 4 (Giving feedback), and Ch. 6 (Relating to Employees with Authenticity and Emotional Intelligence).

Meaningful Work

• •

"Man's search for meaning is the primary motivation in his life".
–Viktor Frankl

• •

In addition to positive communication, another way leaders can ignite their teams is by providing meaningful work.

Assess the extent to which you currently engage your employees through meaningful work using the scale:

Never (N), Rarely (R), Sometimes (S), Often (O) and Always (A)

At the bottom of the table, total the number of times you circle each letter. Consider your pattern:

- Which behaviors are you often or always doing? These indicate areas of strength for you.
- Which behaviors are you never or rarely doing? These indicate behaviors that you should try to do more frequently.

	Meaningful Work
N R S O A	1. I provide my team members with meaningful work.
N R S O A	2. I provide my team members with challenging work.
N R S O A	3. I remind my team members that their jobs are critical to the organization.
N R S O A	4. I assign my team members interesting tasks.
N R S O A	5. I provide my team members with tasks that align with their personal values.
N R S O A	6. I ensure that team members are able to perform their tasks in an optimal work environment.
N R S O A	7. I encourage my team members to support one another.
N R S O A	8. I build trust within my team by being consistent in what I say and do.

• •

"We're here to put a dent in the universe.
Otherwise, why else even be here?"
–Steve Jobs

• •

Why is meaningful work particularly important?

The concept of meaningfulness has been highlighted in a lot of psychological research, most notably by the seminal work on personal engagement conducted by William Kahn.[14] According to Kahn, personal engagement is the extent to which people are able to express and utilize their full selves (cognitively, emotionally and behaviorally) while at work. He found that there are three psychological conditions that determine whether people will be personally engaged or disengaged: *meaningfulness*, *safety* and *availability*. Of these three conditions, meaningfulness is consistently the strongest predictor of engagement; it is also the most relevant to our theme of "igniting."

Meaningfulness refers to being able to do something worthwhile, being able to contribute, and being valued. It comes from both meaningful work and meaningful interactions with others. The following quotations, from Kahn's qualitative research in two different industries, demonstrate how meaningfulness is experienced through task and role characteristics and through connections with other people.

The project I'm working on involves the restoration of a historical building, reconstruction of a demolished historic room, and the addition of a new building along with an old one. That's a lot of complexity, and difficult as projects go. It's also the one that gets me excited about coming into the office. (p. 704)

I would say my involvement comes from individuals. It's an immediate, initial, thing that happens, a connection that I make each time that I work with someone with whom I find some common ground, some shared ways of thinking about things. If I don't have that connection, it's tough for me to get going working with them. (p. 707).

Purpose and fulfillment at work tend to be more important drivers of employee engagement than compensation. For example, 10,000 people were surveyed about which characteristics were critical to a "good job." Results showed that interesting work (86%) and a feeling of accomplishment (76%) were more important than pay (66%) and job security (57%).[15]

Meaningful work seems to be particularly important to the engagement of Millennials. A Gallup report on how Millennials want to work and live showed that they are the least engaged among the generations at work (29%), compared to Gen Xers (32%), Baby Boomers (33%) and Traditionalists (45%). More than half of Millennials are on the lookout for new jobs and new opportunities because they want their work and life to be filled with purpose and meaning. They also want to grow and develop constantly.[16]

Meaningful work can be conceptualized in four different ways, as can be seen in Figure 1.[17]

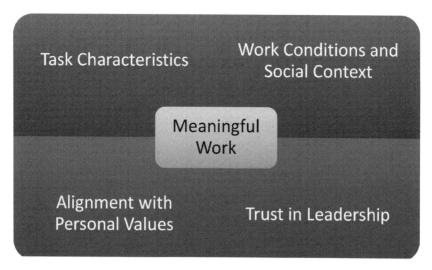

Figure 1.1: Meaningful Work

Task Characteristics.

Meaningful work has some or all of these characteristics. Managers can engage team members by designing work with as many of the following characteristics as possible:

1. Variety – the work involves different types of tasks/activities and employs different skills and competencies
2. Task significance – the job is important and potentially affects other individuals or groups
3. Task identity – the team member can perform a job from beginning to end, and witness a visible outcome
4. Job complexity and problem-solving – the job is sufficiently complex and challenging, often involving problem-solving
5. Task specialization – the work requires distinctive skills for which some amount of training and experience is required
6. Feedback and information processing – the team member sees or receives information about the results of the work and can process the feedback to devise strategies to enhance future performance
7. Autonomy –the team member has discretionary power to decide on his or her own work schedules, work methods and other arrangements.

Reflection:

How can you, as a manager, leverage one or more of these task characteristics to enhance meaningful work within your team?

- A simple group activity could involve assessing and discussing the team's current work against the above seven characteristics using a scale of 1=Very low to 5=Very high). Encourage members to share which tasks or aspects of tasks they find particularly meaningful and which ones they don't find meaningful at all. Then brainstorm ways to inject more meaningfulness through one or more of the seven aspects above.

- Another strategy is to engage in job crafting, which is a process of expanding job boundaries through increased tasks, relationships and cognitive reframing. (See Tool 1.2 for a fuller description).

In your role as a manager, what do you need from the organization that would enhance and support meaningful work within your team? (Because teamwork does not take place in a vacuum, but in the larger context of the organization, consider the kind of support you need to ask for from your leaders and the organization as a whole.)

Work Conditions and Social Context

Work is more likely to be seen as meaningful when accomplished in a physically and socially conducive work setting. Managers can enhance the physical and social environment of their employees in various ways:

1. Provide the requisite tools, technology and other resources to support employee success

2. Invest in ergonomic furniture and equipment as well as attractive, well-lit and well-designed physical workspaces. Research in ergonomics (the science of designing equipment and work arrangements for the purpose of increased efficiency and safety) shows that it is difficult to be engaged in an environment with old or inadequate technology, non-ergonomic furniture, and drab, enclosed spaces. Design companies like Herman Miller have been working with diverse organizations to design cool, new workspaces that build a stronger sense of belonging and overall work engagement. A number of their design innovations include: creating unique and attractive spaces for individual and group work, planning traffic paths and incorporating visual tools like whiteboards, multimedia displays, and tackable surfaces in public areas.

3. Survey your employees to identify a few key amenities that would make a difference to their coming to work each day. However, be careful about promising too much and not delivering; talk rather about feasible options. These may mean a better chair, flexible hours, access to childcare, free parking or discounted transportation. Not all organizations can or want to look like GooglePlex. (Google's Mountain View, California campus, which famously features amenities like gardens, free restaurants, volleyball courts and lots of playful, creative and communal spaces.) Nevertheless, employees do appreciate when their environments are designed to make it easier, more convenient and more fun to work in.

4. Have your employees interact on a regular basis with the people whose work or lives they affect (i.e., internal or external customers and the community at large). By doing so, they get to see the value and impact of their work on others.

5. Encourage team members to collaborate with and learn from one another. Even when team members need to do independent work, schedule periodic meetings so they have opportunities to connect with their peers to solicit feedback, ideas and support.

6. Find ways for team members to get to know one another on a personal basis. They could do things together, whether in support of a meaningful project or charity, or simply to have fun. The more they find areas of shared values, passion and interests, the more they will enjoy working with each other.

Overall, employees are more likely to think of their work as being engaging and meaningful when they enjoy who they are working with, when they believe their managers are supportive, and when the organization provides them with a physically appealing, comfortable and resource-adequate environment. When the organization invests in the requisite social, technological and workplace supports, employees feel they are important and that they themselves are meaningful.

Alignment with personal values

For work to be meaningful, it must link to a broader vision, mission and values set by the organization and its leaders. Moreover, these must align with employees' personal values so that their work allows them not just to strive for the organization's goals, but also to meet their own "calling" or life purpose.[18]

Here are some key questions to ask to see whether the work aligns with team members' personal values:[19]

- Does the work enable the expression of each team member's strengths or best personal capacities?
- Does the work allow each team member to achieve his or her own personal vision?
- Does the work allow team members to learn and grow so that they not only transform themselves but the world around them?
- Does the work ultimately build each team member's self-esteem and self-actualization?

Employees are more likely to be motivated and engaged when they view their current career as a "calling" rather than merely a job.

Case Example – Mother Theresa

Mother Theresa was born in present-day Macedonia, became a Catholic nun and taught in a convent in Calcutta for about 20 years. But the Bengal famine of 1943, which killed more than two million people, left a significant impression on her. She felt "a calling within a calling" to leave her convent and go out to help and feed the poorest of the poor. She eventually formed a new community called the Sisters of Charity that helped orphans, the homeless, people with addiction and victims of disaster, among others. She was recognized with the Nobel Peace Prize and became a Catholic saint.[20]

We don't have to be Mother Theresa to be effective leaders, but the point is: each of us has a calling that will drive and ignite us to achieve bigger, bolder and better things. The best leaders encourage their followers to look inside themselves, identify their values and strengths, and create opportunities for their people to find meaning in their work.

(Refer to Tool 1.3 for more discussion on "career as calling.")

When employees are able to respond to questions like, "Why am I here? Why am I working for Company X?" with "Because I firmly believe in what Company X stands for" and "Because I am able to do the work I am meant to do," they are most likely engaged by their work and committed to their teams.

Trust in leadership

Employee engagement tends to be higher when employees believe in the integrity of their leaders and when they believe their companies as a whole are highly ethical and socially responsible. In fact, a survey conducted by the Society of Human Resource Management showed that 94% of respondents believe that trust between senior leaders and employees is paramount, but only about two-thirds are satisfied about the level of trust within their own organizations.[21] Perhaps some of you received communications from leaders who you did not trust to be honest and sincere. Do you remember rolling your eyes and feeling cynical?

Leaders who are honest and do what they say they will do tend to be viewed as trustworthy. They serve as great role models and sources of inspiration for their employees. Generally, research shows that employees tend to be more engaged in companies that are highly ethical and socially responsible. Working in such companies reinforces employee feelings of pride and loyalty. In contrast, working in companies with unethical leaders breeds feelings of cynicism, anger, embarrassment and shame among employees. Employees will increasingly withdraw their personal investment and efforts in their work and ultimately look for other job opportunities that will satisfy their need for meaning and fulfillment.

In the business context, a contemporary example of an honest and authentic leader is Glenn Kelman, CEO of Redfin, an online real-estate brokerage firm that aims to save customers thousands in agent commissions. When traditional real-estate agents badmouthed the company and started blacklisting customers who used Redfin, Kelman initiated a blog wherein he not only exposed the dirty aspects of the industry, but also critiqued Redfin, and even himself, as a leader. Employees and customers appreciated his candor and honesty, and this contributed to the growth of the business.[22]

Case Example – Dara Khosrowshahi (Uber)

Dara Khosrowshahi was hired in 2017 to be CEO of Uber to replace founder Travis Kalanick after allegations of rampant sexual harassment and discrimination in the ride-hailing giant. Uber was also slammed for not doing enough to prevent and respond to sexual harassment and assault claims committed either by Uber drivers or passengers.

Khosrowshahi is in the midst of reshaping the company image and culture of Uber and rebuilding the trust of its internal stakeholders (its corporate employees and drivers) as well as its external stakeholders (its investors, customers, and the general public). One of his key messages to Silicon Valley was that leaders and tech companies must take more active responsibility monitoring people's usage of their platforms. According to him, it is an ethical responsibility to ensure that people do not use such platforms for abusive and discriminatory behavior.[23]

Khosrowshahi has taken some steps to clean up Uber, such as firing several employees linked with sexual-harassment complaints, hiring more women, and developing a system for tracking and responding to sexual harassment and assault complaints of Uber drivers and riders. In an unusual move, Uber aired a series of national commercials in 2018 where Khosrowshahi talked about wisdom he gained from his father and promised that Uber will be a much better company under his leadership. He faces a difficult challenge to regain trust within his organization and with the public.

Reflection:

Trust is such an elusive phenomenon.

How can you tell if your team trusts you?

Trust is a two-way street. If you are not sure whether your team trusts you, ask yourself these questions:

Do you trust your team? Why or why not?

What does your team need to do in order for you to trust them?

Now, what do you need to do to get your team to trust you?

Here are some steps leaders can take to build trust among employees:[24]

- Check in frequently with your employees (up, down and across the organization).
- Create a safe, positive environment to have conversations about difficult issues.
- Communicate your needs, promises and requests clearly. Keep the door open for negotiation as appropriate.
- Be the first to bring up difficult issues and acknowledge when you may not have the answers.
- Encourage collaborative problem-solving.
- Provide honest feedback, and solicit honest feedback from others.
- Role model respect for others.
- Be appreciative of your employees' honesty and candor.
- When delegating, make sure to "fly air cover" for your team members. This means to allow them to work independently, while providing a safe and supportive space. This is quite a risk for leaders as it may include shielding one's team from external concerns as well as defending team member decisions (and mistakes) to higher authorities.
- Be reliable. Do and deliver as you have promised. If changes need to be made, inform and explain why in an open and timely manner.

Takeaways

Igniting is all about stimulating and energizing your team. Leaders can engage their teams by:

- Communicating in positive and inspiring ways
- Emphasizing the meaningfulness of their employees' work, linking it directly with employees' personal values and needs
- Highlighting the purpose of the team and aligning it with the vision and mission of the organization, and the organization's desired impact on the broader community
- Working proactively to design work roles and support structures to maximize the meaningfulness and engagement potential of employees' jobs
- Acting in ways that demonstrate integrity, thereby building trust within the team and the organization as a whole.

Tool 1.1: Your Engagement "Spark Plugs"

Look at the list below and place a check to the left of the ten factors that most ignite your personal engagement at work. Review these top-ten spark plugs.

Is there a pattern to what you've selected? Are you currently getting enough of these spark plugs at work?

In what ways can you, your manager, and/or the organization as a whole provide you with more of these spark plugs?

This is an exercise you can also invite your team members to do. You can discuss what sparks most, if not all, of you team members.

☐ Autonomy	☐ Interesting work	☐ Positive work climate
☐ Recognition	☐ Meaningful work (making a difference to society)	☐ Authentic leaders
☐ Attractive Base Pay	☐ Task variety	☐ Flexibility
☐ Bonuses	☐ Empowerment	☐ Work safety
☐ Benefits	☐ Inspiring organization vision and mission	☐ Opportunities for cross-training
☐ Supportive relationships with co-workers	☐ Availability of resources and support for work	☐ Innovative culture
☐ Positive relationship with boss	☐ Job and role clarity	☐ High-trust work relationships
☐ Personal growth and development opportunities	☐ Career-advancement opportunities	☐ Job-person fit
☐ Opportunities to use one's skills and strengths at work	☐ Collaborative team environment	☐ Challenging work
☐ Coaching and mentoring	☐ Opportunity to leave a legacy through one's work	☐ Rewarding social interactions with people
☐ Stock options	☐ Feelings of inclusion and belongingness	☐ Clear communication of goals and direction
☐ Work-life balance	☐ Ability to enhance self-efficacy (confidence)	☐ Reasonable work demands
☐ Job security	☐ Inspiring leaders	☐ Feelings of personal accomplishment
☐ Ability to fulfill one's life purpose and goals	☐ Efficient work systems and structures	☐ Opportunity to self-actualize
☐ Integrity of organizational leaders	☐ Accountability for performance	☐ Fun work environment

Tool 1.2: Job Crafting

Job crafting is a process where employees actively modify the formal aspects of their jobs to better suit their strengths, interests and passions.* The job-crafting process helps employees and managers make jobs more engaging and fulfilling, enhance overall job performance, and increase employees' resilience to adversity.

Here are some ways managers can help their people craft their jobs to make them more engaging:

a. Task crafting – Add or reduce job tasks; increase or decrease scope of responsibilities; change the way the employee performs tasks

b. Relational crafting – Change with whom and how much the employee interacts with others (e.g., computer programmer who feels that there isn't enough interaction with others. They could be encouraged to regularly visit co-workers to provide help and also get feedback on computer systems)

c. Cognitive crafting – Shift how the employee views the task, focusing on the meaning and impact of the task (e.g., janitor in a hospital seeing the job of cleaning as a fundamental way of helping people to heal). Think about a series of tedious tasks as a collective whole (e.g., insurance agent seeing the job as "helping people recover after a car accident" rather than processing insurance claims).

d. Combination of the above

Take out a sheet of paper and make a list of job crafting steps that you and your team member(s) could consider. What benefits would the employee and the team as a whole gain by making these changes?

Note: In actuality, people engage in job crafting whether they or their managers know it or not. Thus, it is important that managers work openly with their employees to ensure that changes to the job will not result in unintended issues such as misalignment with team or organizational goals, additional stress and distractions.

* Wrzesniewski, A. & Dutton, J. E. (2001). Crafting a job: Revisioning employees as active crafters of their work. Academy of Management Review, 26 (2), 179-201.

Tool 1.3: Career versus Calling

People will find more meaning in their jobs when they view it as a "calling" rather than a career. While it is naïve to say that most of us will end up in jobs that we were truly "born to do", this should not mean that we allow ourselves to get stuck in jobs we hate, but consider to be the more "practical" routes.

Here are some questions to reflect on and help us identify which activities and jobs "call" to us at a deeper level.* Managers can also use these questions when having discussions with their employees. (See also Tool 1.2 for a related activity called job crafting.)

What do you love to do?

What lights you up?

What activities would you keep on doing even if you weren't paid for them?

In which types of activities do you find yourself fully engrossed, losing track of time, and essentially being in a state of "flow"?

What could you be doing or talking about for hours on end?

What do you enjoy learning about even if you didn't have to?

Does your current job provide you with at least 50% of the types of activities that ignite you?

Are you able to describe to others the meaning and purpose of your job in ways that feel "true" to your own identity and life's purpose? Is there a clear connection between your work's purpose and your life's calling? Is it easy for you to verbalize this?

Are you able to describe the contributions to others and society in general that you are making through your job?

If your job doesn't allow you to do what you love to do, or express yourself in ways you wish to do so more than 50% of the time, are there ways you can inject more of the things you love into it?

Alternatively, are there other venues (non-job related) for you to express your calling without interfering with your formal job responsibilities? (For example, your company might allow you to do the things you love as a benefit, e.g., volunteer at a charity for a specific number of days a year). Perhaps you can't apply your creativity very much at work; however, you find non-work outlets for it — being a member of an amateur dramatics society or attending art/pottery/dancing/photoshop classes.)

If your job doesn't allow you to fulfill your true "calling", have you looked at other departments / organizations that offer more opportunities for you to do so?

* Butzer, B. (2013). Career vs. calling: Is there a difference? Retrieved from https://www.positivelypositive.com/2013/07/14/career-vs-calling-is-there-a-difference/

Chapter 2

Nurture Your People

"Help them grow or watch them go."
–Mike Martin, Ingersoll Rand

How would you react if one of your employees told you that she wished to leave your organization? We suppose the answer is: "It depends!"

- If the employee hasn't been particularly productive, or has created problems and conflicts, you're probably happy that she is going to leave.
- But supposing this is one of your star employees and she cites lack of development as the key reason for leaving. What would you do?

Throughout this chapter, you will find many suggestions to handle this situation; and by using some of these strategies, you may be able to persuade your employee to stay. In fact, when you apply these tactics, your employee may not get to the stage of wanting to leave your organization in the first place! On the other hand – especially with a star performer – maybe this is the time you should let go and support your employee as she move to the next stage of her career. Maybe it's a time to sponsor talent rather than hoard it.

Employee growth and career development is crucial in today's working environment. The unemployment rate in the USA is at an all-time low, and job automation continues to grow, resulting in the specialization of future job-related skills. It's no wonder that the "opportunity to learn" is high on the list of reasons cited by both Millennials and "Gen Z" when considering a company for employment.[1]

Nurture

To nurture is to tend to someone during their growth/development – to support, train, educate, nourish and encourage them. Effective managers and leaders do nurture their employees – they foster the learning and development of their direct reports. You could say that this whole book is about nurturing – nurturing success, leadership and engagement. However, in this chapter, we'll be focusing on just one aspect of nurturing – career development.

Rather than being bored and restless at work, employees like to have a job in which they can make full use of their skills. Nurturing your team members helps them reach their full potential as they are developing at work, learning new skills and continually growing. Their self-esteem increases as they feel they make a difference, impacting the people they serve and contributing to the goals of the organization. When employees feel that they're preparing themselves for the future, they're engaged and committed to the organization. As you will see further on in this chapter, growth and development opportunities are especially important to Millennials.

Before reading further, assess your nurturing / employee development skills by completing the survey below, using the scale:

Never (N), Rarely (R), Sometimes (S), Often (O) and Always (A)

At the bottom of the table, total the number of times you circle each letter. Consider your pattern:

- Which behaviors are you often or always doing? These indicate areas of strength for you.
- Which behaviors are you never or rarely doing? These suggest behaviors that you should try to do more frequently.

Rating	Nurture / Employee Development
N R S O A	1. I know my team members' skills and capabilities
N R S O A	2. I know my team members' career aspirations.
N R S O A	3. I encourage my team members to take advantage of our organization's training and development opportunities.
N R S O A	4. I provide on-the-job learning opportunities to my team members.
N R S O A	5. I provide my team members with the resources necessary to support their professional development.

N R S O A	6. I have regular career development conversations with my team members.

Relationship Between Employee Engagement, Retention and Career Development

Career development enhances both retention and employee engagement.

Retention – the intention of employees to stay with their current organization – is an indication of how strongly committed they are to the company, an aspect of engagement. A global workforce study showed that one of the key reasons people joined – and stayed with – their companies was for career advancement.[2] Additionally, the lack of career advancement came in second as the reason workers resign. This is supported by a more recent study – a 2019 Retention Report – which identified career development as the number one reason employees left their jobs. It constituted 22% of all the reasons people quit.[3] Other research reported that 33% of the professionals surveyed stated that the main reason they were planning to look for a new job was because they were currently bored as they weren't being sufficiently challenged.[4]

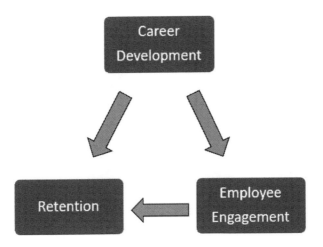

Figure 2.1: Relationship between Career Development, Retention and Employee Engagement

There is also a correlation between career development and employee engagement. A study compared organizations based on their level of engagement – high, average or low engagement.[5] They found that in highly engaged organizations, 73% of employees agreed that they had the opportunity to grow and develop in their positions (versus only 43% in organizations with low levels of engagement). Moreover, 69% of employees from highly engaged organizations agreed that they had career opportunities in their company (versus only 38% of employees in organizations with low levels of engagement). In another study, 45% of Millennials (versus 31% of Gen Xers and 18% of Baby Boomers) said that a position that fast-tracks their growth and career development is important to them.[6]

Millennials value development more than any other generation. In one study, 87% of Millennials stated that development at work was highly valued in a new position and was an important reason for them to stay at their current organization.[7] This opportunity for growth, for learning something new (and meaningful) at work is a critical factor in recruiting and retaining them. Is your organization leveraging this aspect of engagement, especially with Millennials?

An effective career management program/strategy is key in increasing employee loyalty, motivation, engagement and retention.

See Tool 2.1 – Checklist (Are You a Nurturing Manager?) at the end of the chapter for a comprehensive list of actions that nurturing managers take. How nurturing are you with your employees? How many items can you check off?

Case Example – T-Mobile [8]

Here is an example demonstrating how career development affected employee turnover and engagement.

T-Mobile has 52,000 employees. The company wanted to reduce employee turnover – especially amongst its front-line care and retail workers. They also wanted to establish a more transparent career development program as many of these frontline employees were confused about their career prospects and had the impression that few development and promotional opportunities were available.

T-Mobile created a "Career Success" campaign over many months and featured CareerFest – a week-long online career fair. Participants were able to ask questions in live interactive chat rooms. Activities included job exploration and career guidance, the ability to audition for future job shadowing and opportunities to meet career advocates. During that first week, over 9,000 employees participated in the Career Success program.

CareerFest participants applied for internal roles and experienced growth transfers at rates that were significantly higher than those employees who did not participate in the event. In addition, employee awareness of their career-development prospects increased, employee turnover decreased, and productivity improved. (Notably, the cost of the program was just $1.86 per attendee.)

Your organization may not be able to develop an extensive program like T-Mobile's Career Success campaign. However, there are a number of elements of this program that you could implement (or champion your company to implement), to enhance the growth and career-development prospects of your team members, thereby increasing retention and productivity. Several of these components are addressed later in this chapter (e.g., regular career-focused discussions with your team members in which you determine your employee's career aspirations and explore other opportunities within your department and within the organization).

The Changing World of Career Development

Career development occurs when a company facilitates the career growth of its employees by providing opportunities for education, skill development (technical, professional, personal and managerial), coaching and cross-training. "Job security ... depends on building and maintaining a set of skills and experiences that employers need. To individuals, this acquisition and development of skills and experiences is what constitutes a career in today's environment." [9]

Historically, career development has focused on the upward path/trajectory in an organization. Employees used to remain in the same organization for many years. They started at the company with little or no experience and worked their way up the career ladder. There were specific career paths for each kind of position (engineer, administrator, etc.). Employees knew approximately how many years it would take to get from one rung of the ladder to the next one. Sometimes, there were lateral moves (merely to obtain broader experience), but the goal was usually to reach the top echelon of the organization – to be promoted up into the "C" suite.

The world of work has changed considerably over the last twenty years, with mergers and acquisitions, downsizing and numerous lay-offs. Organizations are perceived as not being loyal to their workforce. Because of this, employees no longer feel an obligation to stay with their organizations for twenty or thirty years, as they did in the past. There is much more of a "cut-and-run" attitude. "You are paying me for the work I'm doing right now. That is our contract – that's the only loyalty!" As longevity doesn't seem to be supported by organizations, employees don't feel disloyal if they leave the company after a short time. Their thinking is: "As an employee, I don't trust that you'll take care of me in the long term, so – besides giving you my best while I'm here – I'm also going to add to my marketability by learning as much as I can, which will increase my employability at any organization."

The older generations – the baby boomers and traditionalists – may still think that they shouldn't job-hop. However, the younger generations don't have a problem with it. Gallup found that 60% of Millennials are open to job change, with 36% of them looking for an opportunity with a different company.[10] This is higher than the non-Millennials – 45% are open to a job change, and 21% looking for a position in a different organization. In even better economic times, the percentage of employees open to job change would probably increase.

In addition to the above, companies are now leaner. Many middle management positions have been eliminated, resulting in the flattening of organizational structures with markedly fewer advancement opportunities than before. Because there are fewer managers, this may mean that employees have more autonomy at work; however, it also means that promotional opportunities, especially into management, are more infrequent. This is detrimental for employees who want to move up the ladder as managerial experience is an essential skill. Also, as higher positions require broader experience – which they can't necessarily find in internal candidates – companies often hire externally. This can lead to frustration for employees (especially those high potentials who were expecting a promotion) who then conclude that there aren't/won't be future career development opportunities within their current organization.

Rather than just the conventional idea of career progression – the traditional career ladder -- there is now also the concept of a career lattice.[11] This new framework provides various lateral professional development experiences, resulting in tailored zig-zagging career paths. In this contemporary approach, rather than a focus on promotions, title and power, intrinsic aspects of work are highlighted: more effective utilization of talents and skills, challenging work that contributes to professional growth, and the ability to make an impact.

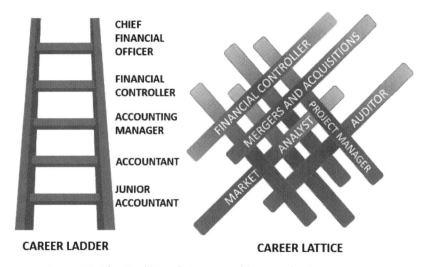

CAREER LADDER

CHIEF
FINANCIAL
OFFICER

FINANCIAL
CONTROLLER

ACCOUNTING
MANAGER

ACCOUNTANT

JUNIOR
ACCOUNTANT

CAREER LATTICE

FINANCIAL CONTROLLER

MERGERS AND ACQUISITIONS

MARKET ANALYST PROJECT MANAGER AUDITOR

Figure 2.2: The Traditional Career Ladder Vs. The Contemporary Career Lattice

Because of these changes in the arena of career development, there has been a shift from career advancement to personal growth and development. Now, organizations and leaders need to support each employee in career growth – which doesn't necessarily mean a vertical promotion, but may instead be a lateral move. In fact, some employees may request a lateral or downward career move, if it supports their current need for more work/life balance or long-term career aspirations. This is especially true for employees who have been promoted into a supervisory/managerial position, but then realize that managing others isn't motivating or engaging – they'd rather be an individual contributor. Previous career planning frameworks are outdated. In the current more ambiguous career environment, companies need to define the new indicators that employees can use on their personal career path as they maneuver their way around the organization in today's fluid career landscape.

Case Example – Career Management[12]

In the finance division of a global retail firm, staff weren't being developed for advancement into the higher levels of the organization. The organization continually hired external candidates with broader experience. This was troubling to employees – especially the high potential ones – and resulted in low engagement and low morale.

To overcome these employee concerns, the company introduced some new career growth strategies. They identified the competencies and skills needed in both generalist and specialized career paths and offered new career development opportunities. Managers were given career coaching training so they could assist their employees in determining skill gaps and establishing career development goals. Job rotation was introduced so employees could move laterally and develop a broader skillset.

As the organization now largely promotes internal candidates, retention and employee engagement has increased.

Rewards

We don't address extrinsic rewards in this book. There are two reasons for this. Firstly, compensation planning is not part of our expertise – there are other resources where you can find up-to-date information. Secondly, although salary and compensation are obviously important in driving the engagement of employees, it's not necessarily number one, especially with Millennials. One study found that although high compensation (and a positive corporate culture) might attract Millennials, it was inclusion/diversity and flexibility that drove engagement and retention.1 In addition, Millennials strive for work that has a purpose and work/life balance.[10] However, even though the opportunity for career development may be perceived by employees as more of an intrinsic reward, this career growth could lead to extrinsic rewards such as progressive promotions and higher compensation.

Effective Career Development: Who is Responsible for it?

In today's workplace, giving your team members training and career development and growth opportunities is not a perk – it's a necessity if you want your employees to be engaged and fully committed to achieving the goals of your organization.

The ideal situation occurs when an employee's ambitions correspond with the future talent needs of the company. The closer the match between these two components, the greater the win-win or in this case, the win-win-win.

Career development/management is a **three-way** collaboration:

- The manager is the coach/facilitator.
- The individual is the driver of the process.
- The organization provides the support system.

It's a victory for all parties when the employee's career objectives align with the skills/abilities/experience needed to fill future positions in the organization. In this situation, the employee works effectively and is inspired to continue his growth and development and be ready for any opportunities that arise; the leader has engaged employees who fulfill their current obligations and who are motivated to accept new assignments; and the company has the committed talent it needs, both to achieve current goals, and to step up to the plate when staffing gaps occur.

Visualize it as a Venn diagram — the "sweet spot" (area #7) – is where there is an overlap of all three components:

Figure 2.3: Relationship of Employee, Manager and the Organization

In this sweet spot (#7):

- *Employees* are fully engaged and highly productive, as they are doing work they love (their purpose is in alignment with the organization's mission), and they're achieving their career goals. (Perhaps their career plan is that they want a promotion, or a lateral move to another department so they can learn new skills and add to their marketability). Their manager and the organization provide ample training and development opportunities for them.

- *The manager* is happy, both with the employee's current performance, and his ambition to enhance his skills and develop to the next level. The manager can rely on the employee's work commitment and knows he will step in where there is a gap (e.g., when the manager or other employees are on vacation, or if the manager leaves the department or company). The leader has frequent conversations with individual employees, focusing on their career plans, and ensuring the employees understand how the organization's and department's goals align with the employees' goals.

- *The organization* has a satisfied and productive manager and motivated and engaged team members. If the leader is transferred/promoted to another department or unexpectedly leaves the company, another employee can step in temporarily and fill in for the manager (and may be able to take this position permanently). If the organization expands and needs a worker like one of these employees in a new branch (either as an individual contributor or a manager), they have someone they know is an effective worker who values the organization's mission and knows the culture.

It's a win-win-win all around!

DEEPER DIVE

How can the "sweet spot" (area #7) be boosted?

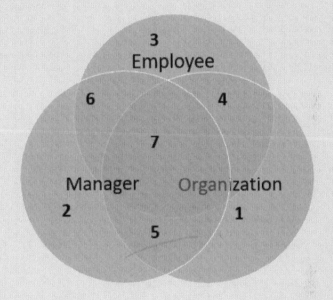

The sweet spot (area 7) can be enlarged if the overlapping areas (4, 5 & 6) can be expanded.

- Area 4 – between the organization and the employee – can be increased by ensuring that the purpose and values of the employee are in alignment with the mission and values of the organization. (This is addressed initially in the recruiting and onboarding processes.) The more the employee feels that the organization is trustworthy and cares for its employees, providing ample development and growth opportunities and allowing him to take risks, the more engaged and committed the employee will be.

- Area 5 – between the organization and the manager – can be increased by the same items as in Area 4 (after all, the leader is an employee too). Can the manager trust that the organization keeps its promises, cares for its employees, and is fair regarding promotional opportunities?

- Area 6 – between the manager and the employee – can be increased when the leader is effective at motivating and engaging her team members, providing effective performance management and ample career development opportunities. The employee also needs to hold up his side of the "bargain" by achieving departmental goals and supporting the leader's initiatives.

As the leader, how can you enhance these three areas of overlap, so the sweet spot is larger and the wins for all parties are increased?

Manager's Responsibilities (The Coach/Facilitator)

Some managers think that they don't have enough time (along with all their other priorities) to focus on the careers of their direct reports. It's important to remember that there are enormous benefits to you, the leader – increased loyalty and retention, and team members who are better-prepared to step in at the last minute if the need arises.

It seems that it is a worthwhile investment, as career development is amongst the top drivers for employee engagement (especially with Millennials). In addition, the fact that you're reading this book means that you want to become more effective at engaging your team. Nurturing personal growth and development is the answer.

Reflection:

Think about your working experience – which supervisor/leader has helped your career growth? How?

How was your engagement affected when this manager supported your career growth and development?

Now think about a supervisor/leader who did not support your career growth.

How was your engagement affected when this manager wasn't supportive of your career growth and development?

From your experience, which specific/effective strategies can you adapt/use as you work on the career development of your current team members? Take a look at Tool 2.1 – Checklist – Are You a Nurturing Manager? – for additional ideas.

Your Relationship with Your Employee

Research demonstrates that the relationship between the direct report and manager is critical in enhancing employee satisfaction, engagement and productivity. The leader should get to know each employee on an individual (and personal) basis, and learn about their strengths, their likes and dislikes and their career aspirations. How do you keep track of this information? Many companies now have software programs enabling you to capture this data online. If you don't have this capability, you just might have to use pencil and paper to create a profile for each team member, summarizing this information. One author suggests creating a spreadsheet for each of your employees, to include information such as the employee's preferred method of working, their key motivators, your own observations of their work, etc..[13] It's essential to collaborate with each employee to assist in creating their individual career development plan, to have regular development discussions, and to provide them with necessary resources. Are your employee's ambitions aligned with organizational opportunities? What could you do to ensure a closer alignment? It is your responsibility to encourage your direct reports to take advantage of any educational / growth opportunities offered by the company, as well as to provide realistic expectations about advancement. How often do you have a career-focused discussion with your team members? In most organizations, these meetings occur – if at all – just once a year. However, 77.5% of employees would like to have quarterly career conversations with their managers.[14]

Look at Tool 2.1: Checklist – Are You a Nurturing Manager? which includes ideas on how you can be an effective, nurturing leader

Coaching Around Training

Supervisory support and coaching are essential, especially in relation to training (see Chapter 4 for a detailed discussion on coaching).

- When a team member has scheduled training, have a pre-training meeting with her. Some discussion questions might include:

- □ What is the goal of the training?
- □ How will this training enable you to achieve your work goals more effectively?
- □ How will this training enable you to achieve your career goals?
- □ What are your expectations about the training?
- □ How will you implement what you will learn when you return to work?
- □ How can I best support you before, during and after the training?

- Additionally, have a post-training follow-up discussion with the employee. How can you help your employee clarify her learning and focus on a few specific behaviors she can implement right away? Some discussion questions might include:
  - □ What was your experience during the training program?
  - □ What is your plan for applying your learning?
  - □ How have you implemented your learning since returning to work?
  - □ Are there any obstacles that may prevent you from fully applying your learning?
  - □ Would you recommend this training for others in the department? Why/why not?
  - □ What additional support can I provide?
  - □ From what you learned, how will this training help you to achieve your career goals?
  - □ How can you best share your learning with your colleagues?

Make sure you give your team members feedback when you notice they've changed their behavior and/or implemented what they learned. These strategies apply whether the employees participated in a workshop, attended a conference, or were involved in online or mobile-ready learning. In addition, this is also an ideal opportunity for employees to learn from each other – have the recently trained employee share her new knowledge/skills with her team members.

Job Enrichment

Because you, as the leader, are the one who knows the employee and the job tasks, you can provide challenging (stretch) activities for your team member. These assignments provide the opportunity for the employee to try his hand at something new, perhaps slightly beyond his current level of skills/knowledge. It enables him to develop and demonstrate competence in a different area. Up is not the only way. Because of the shortage of vertical movement opportunities, managers (and employees) need to find a different way to add excitement and challenge to work. How can the current position be enriched or redesigned? How can the job content be re-crafted so the team member can focus on areas which best utilize her talents and strengths? (See Chapter 1 for more on job crafting.) You can also determine how job responsibilities could be augmented. An effective way of tapping into employee engagement and building a more cohesive team is to redistribute tasks amongst your employees in alignment with their strengths and passions. If it's possible to change tasks and re-craft jobs in this way, your team members will be happier and more productive, which is that win-win-win situation mentioned above.

• •

"Think of your employees as diamonds in the rough. It's your job to nurture them and help them shine brightly."
–Pearl Hilliard

• •

Championing Growth and Development

As a leader in your company, it's essential that you support your organization's career development practices/policies. Be a champion of learning, growth and career development. This means that you allow your employees time away from their work so they can utilize educational or developmental opportunities offered by your company. (It is also motivating for other team members to see their colleagues being given growth and development opportunities.) Unfortunately, it means that you need to accept that some of your employees (and probably your best ones!) will move to other departments or organizations. You should support them in their move – maybe even encourage them to take advantage of lateral or promotional opportunities. It is a huge loss when a star performer moves on, but your responsibility as a leader is to be the platform from which your employees can launch to their next career adventure. This is being an effective leader and mentor. It will also be motivating to your other team members, when they observe that you support employees when they want to move on – rather than berating or ostracizing them. Your other direct reports know you "have their backs" and their best interests at heart.

Another way of looking at the situation is as an opportunity to shake things up – a chance for you and the team to take a strategic look at departmental goals and decide if/how team roles could be reconfigured. How has the team been evolving (or should be evolving) to meet future organizational objectives? Does this give other team members an opportunity to take on new responsibilities? If the team is being revamped, then the replacement employee can be recruited to meet the needs of this new team.[15]

Speaking of mentoring, you could also participate in a mentoring program if your organization has one. Even if they don't, mentor some people in your company (including employees who are not your direct reports). This is a big piece of your nurturing responsibility, and it is part of the legacy you leave behind. Besides assisting your mentees in their career advancement, mentoring also has advantages for the mentor: increased job satisfaction, a loyal support base, career rejuvenation, organizational recognition and the development of new skills. Being a mentor is part of <u>your</u> learning, growth and career development. In addition, you never know if that previous team member may assist you in your career growth. If you've had a good relationship and been supportive of your mentees, they may think of you when an opportunity arises at their new company.

Reflection:

What have you done in the last quarter to support the development of your direct reports?

If you supervise other managers, how do you hold them accountable for the development of their employees?

Review your responses to Tool 2.1 – Checklist – Are You a Nurturing Manager? Select a couple of items that you're not currently doing and create goals around implementing those behaviors.

DEEPER DIVE

Resource: 9-Box Performance-Potential Matrix

We'd like to introduce you to a potential/performance matrix. The author of the 9-box framework isn't known, and there are many adaptations of this popular model. This tool is used frequently in career development and succession planning. HR representatives and managers meet to discuss each employee and agree on the box in which they would <u>currently</u> place each person. Those employees who are deemed "high potential" are perceived to have future leadership aptitude and are then often groomed by their organizations for promotion into leadership positions.

Here is our adaptation of this 9-box tool. In the description of each box, we've provided questions/strategies you can use to maximize the performance and potential of your employee.

Talent Development Matrix

POTENTIAL		**7. PARADOX** • Underperformer • Maybe in the wrong role • Maybe bad fit with manager	**8. FUTURE STAR** • Achieves goals • Valued contributor • Potential for growth	**9. SUPER STAR** • Exceeds targets • Future leader • Strong candidate for promotion
	HIGH POTENTIAL	• What's impeding their performance? • Change role/manager? • Coach – performance manage*; offboard if no improvement	• Challenge – provide leadership and stretch assignments • Provide a mentor • Reward and engage	• Provide special development opportunities • Reward and recognize • Challenge and engage
		4. UNDER-PERFORMER • Underperformer • Obstacles to performance? • Questionable fit	**5. KEY PLAYER** • Achieves goals • Some potential for growth • Needs greater challenges	**6. CURRENT STAR** • Exceeds targets • Valued contributor • Potential for growth
	EVOLVING POTENTIAL	• What's impeding their performance? • Challenge them • Coach – performance manage*; offboard if no improvement	• Provide coaching and development opportunities • Provide stretch assignments	• Actively develop for next level • Provide a mentor • Provide development and growth opportunities

70

		1. MARGINAL	2. SOLID PERFORMER	3. FUNCTIONAL EXPERT
POTENTIAL	REACHED POTENTIAL	• Underperformer • Unlikely to improve	• Achieves goals • Steady contributor • Content with status quo	• Exceeds targets • Loves job • Content with status quo
		• Performance manage*; offboard if no improvement	• Motivate and engage • Discuss their future goals • Provide resources for consistent performance	• Engage, challenge and reward • Discuss their future goals • Can mentor others, share their knowledge
		LOW Unacceptable	AVERAGE Meets expectations	HIGH Exceeds expectations
		PERFORMANCE		

Performance manage: Have a performance discussion with the employee – see Chapter 4 – Performance Management – for more details.

Keep in mind that this is fluid, and the position of the employee in the grid can change, depending on his specific circumstances, his motivation, and what the organization can provide.

Some examples:

- An employee might be caring for a sick family member or an elderly parent and thus not want to take on any additional responsibilities right now – so he has been deemed to fall into box #2 or #3. However, when circumstances change and he can then focus more fully on work, he may well move into box #5 or #6, or even #8 or #9.

- It could be that the employee lacks confidence in her abilities and is too nervous to apply for a promotion. However, if you effectively coach the employee and provide opportunities – small steps – to take on additional responsibilities/try out new behaviors, the employee may begin to see that she has the ability to do more and have potential for further career growth.

As the leader, you need to be aware of the changing circumstances/ambitions of your employees and be flexible in the strategies you use to nurture their talent and careers.

Leaders can independently use this tool to identify the current performance level and potential of their direct reports. As this chapter is focused on nurturing and career development, we're concentrating on boxes 2, 3, 5, 6, 8 and 9. (The sub-par performers – Boxes 1, 4 and 7 – will be addressed in the Performance Management section of Chapter 4.)

Boxes 2 and 3 include employees who have already reached their potential.

- However, those in Box 2, the Solid Performers are the steady contributors. Even though they've reached their potential, and so seem unlikely to progress further at this time, they achieve their goals and make sure everything runs smoothly. You still need to motivate and engage them, reward them for their steady goal achievement, and coach and develop them to achieve higher performance levels. Continue to provide the necessary resources so they can maintain their consistent performance. It is important to have a discussion with them about their future goals and what they want next in their career.

- Those in Box 3, the Functional Experts, are excellent workers who are exceeding their performance targets and so are very valuable contributors in their departments. It's essential to retain these employees through rewarding, engaging and challenging them. As they're so good at their job, they would be ideal for mentoring/training other employees (if that's something they want to do). They are satisfied with their current position and don't seem interested in moving up the ladder (at the moment); however, you still need to have a discussion with them about what else they'd like from their job or the organization – what would they like to achieve next?

Boxes 5 and 6 include employees who have evolving potential.

- Employees in Box 5 are the Key Players – they currently reach their targets, and they have some potential for growth. To help them get to the next level (both in terms of potential and performance), they need to be challenged – stretch assignments will be good here. Also, coaching and development opportunities ought to be provided.

- Employees in Box 6 are Current Stars, as they are high performers who exceed expectations and have potential for more growth. Actively develop these employees for promotion to the next level by providing coaching, a mentor, and stretch assignments.

Boxes 8 and 9 include employees who have high potential.

- Employees in Box 8 are valued contributors as they achieve their goals and have high potential for growth. Provide challenging options for them – stretch assignments and leadership opportunities. It is important to motivate and engage these Future Stars
- Employees in Box 9 are the Super Stars – as well as having high potential, they are your best performers and future leaders. You want to retain these employees, but they are strong candidates for promotion – if there's nowhere in your department for advancement, you will have to support them in their transfer to a different department, or in their move to another organization. While they're with you, you ought to reward and recognize their efforts and engage them by providing challenging opportunities.

Look at Tool 2.2 – Talent Development Matrix. This Performance/Potential matrix has space for you to write in your employees' names in the appropriate box. As you prepare for your career development discussions with your team members, you can review these strategies and decide on the most appropriate ones for each employee.

Employee (The Driver):

Employees are responsible for their own career development. (Remember, you are also an employee.) Before reading further, review the statements below to assess how you are doing regarding your own career development.

- [ ] I know my own skills and capabilities.
- [ ] I have a career development plan.
- [ ] I take advantage of any learning/development opportunities offered by my organization.
- [ ] I know how I'm uniquely contributing to my team/organization.
- [ ] I ensure I have career-related discussions with my manager.
- [ ] I have a mentor.

As an employee, you need to know your own strengths and the value you are providing to your team/your organization. In addition, create a career development plan for yourself so you know where you are going. Regularly speak with your manager about your aspirations and career goals. When taking advantage of any educational, learning or growth opportunities offered by your organization, speak with your leader beforehand so you know his expectations of what you'll be bringing back to the department. After the training, ensure you meet with your manager to discuss how you will implement your new knowledge/skills/abilities. Discuss how you can try out the new behaviors and ask for feedback. In addition, share your new knowledge with your colleagues.

Find a mentor for yourself – it may be your leader or someone else in your organization or someone in the same field of expertise as you (perhaps someone you met through a professional organization).

Again – up is not the only way. Do you recognize the changing nature of the workplace, and appreciate that lateral moves may be how you will acquire different skills and abilities that will support your career plan? Also, perhaps your current job can be re-crafted so you are working with your strengths and finding more "flow" in your work (see Chapter 3 for more on this). Are there ways you can change your current working methods, to be more challenged and achieve higher engagement? Can you focus more on the tasks related to your strengths and passions? Can you exchange pieces of your job with another team member? Can you change how parts of your work are done (while still fulfilling your job duties)?

Reflection:

- *How do you think each of your employees would respond to the questions in Tool 2.3 – Employee Career Development Checklist?*
- *As a manager, you are also an employee. How are you driving your own career development? See Tool 2.3 – Employee Career Development Checklist – a comprehensive checklist, which you can use to determine what you are currently doing well and where you could boost your career development opportunities.*
- *Develop a career / professional development plan for yourself. (If your organization doesn't have an applicable process, see Tool 2.4 – Career Development Action Plan Instructions – and Tool 2.5 – Career Development Action Plan).*

DEEPER DIVE

Organization Support System

The third piece of effective career development is how the organization supports you in your nurturing endeavors. Tool 2.6 – Checklist – Elements of Successful Career Development Programs –provides a list of the kinds of components that determine the success of a career development program. Organizations don't necessarily have all the elements, but it gives you some idea of strategies used in effective career development programs. Perhaps your company doesn't have a robust system. You may not have the authority to change the career development program in your organization. However, maybe there are ways you could influence your company to begin to implement some of these initiatives?

Reflection:

- *Do you have a mentoring program in your organization? If not, how can you informally mentor employees?*
- *How would you rate your organization's career management program? Assess your organization using the Tool 2.6 – Checklist – Elements of Successful Career Development Programs.*

- *Are there any items on this list that you could influence your leaders to implement?*
- *How can you champion career development in your company?*

Reflection:

Now that we're at the end of this chapter, why not re-visit the question we posed earlier:

How would you react if one of your employees wishes to leave and cites lack of development as a key reason? What would you do?

However, as mentioned earlier – if your employee is going to leave no matter what, then support them in their move!

Career development is strongly correlated with employee motivation and engagement. If organizations want to attract and keep high-performing individuals (especially Millennials), it is essential that growth and development opportunities are available. Are you using some of the strategies discussed in this chapter to nurture your team members' growth and development?

Takeaways

- Career development enhances motivation, retention and employee engagement.
- Lack of career development is the number one reason employees quit their jobs.
- Millennials value development more than any other generation.
- Responsibility for career development is three-way – the employee is the driver, the manager is the coach/facilitator, and the organization provides the support system.
- An effective career management program/strategy is key in increasing employee loyalty, motivation, engagement and retention.
- Use some of the strategies discussed in this chapter to nurture your direct reports' growth and development.
- Nurture your own career.

Tool 2.1: Checklist – Are You a Nurturing Manager?

The nurturing manager serves as the coach/facilitator of career development. How nurturing are you with your employees? How many items can you check off? Review the items you are doing. How can you do these even more effectively? Of the elements you are currently not doing, select two or three behaviors you will start doing, and create an action plan around these behaviors.

Do you:

- [ ] Effectively manage the talents and skills of your team members?
- [ ] Get to know each employee on an individual basis?
- [ ] Know their skills and capabilities?
- [ ] Know their values?
- [ ] Have regular meetings with each employee and know their career aspirations?
- [ ] Collaborate with each employee in creating an individual career development plan?
- [ ] Focus on the alignment between your employee's passions and values and those of the organization?
- [ ] Point out the connection / alignment between your employee's ambitions and organizational opportunities?
- [ ] Reinforce a closer alignment?
- [ ] Highlight how they make an impact on the team, department, organization and community?
- [ ] Provide challenging (stretch) activities to your employees, which contribute to their professional growth?
- [ ] Ensure your employees learn from each other?

- [ ] Provide support and coaching to employees, especially relating to training:
  - ○ Encourage your direct reports to take advantage of any educational/growth opportunities offered by the company?
  - ○ Allow employees time away from work so they can utilize training and development opportunities?
  - ○ When an employee goes to training, do you have a pre-training discussion regarding the goal of the training, and how they will implement what they've learned when they return to work?
  - ○ Have a post-training follow-up discussion with your employee – what was the employee's experience during the training program? How have they implemented their learning since returning to work? Give feedback on their new behavior/learning?
  - ○ Encourage them to share this new information with their colleagues?
- [ ] Determine if there are ways to re-craft the job tasks of your employees so they can focus on areas which best utilize their talents and strengths?
- [ ] Provide employees with necessary resources?
- [ ] Provide realistic expectations about advancement?
- [ ] Support them when they move on (either inside or outside the company)?

In addition:

- [ ] Do you support your organization's career development practices/policies?
- [ ] Do you participate in a mentoring program if your organization has one; if not, then mentor some people in your organization (including employees who are not your direct reports)?
- [ ] Are you held accountable for the development of your direct reports?

Tool 2.2: Talent Development Matrix

This Performance/Potential matrix has space for you to write in your employees' names in the appropriate box. You can then review the strategies and decide on the most appropriate ones for each employee as you carry out your career development discussions and plans with the employee.

Talent Development Matrix

			7. PARADOX • Underperformer • Maybe in the wrong role • Maybe bad fit with manager	8. FUTURE STAR • Achieves goals • Valued contributor • Potential for growth	9. SUPER STAR • Exceeds targets • Future leader • Strong candidate for promotion
POTENTIAL	HIGH POTENTIAL		**EMPLOYEE NAMES:** 1. 2. 3.	**EMPLOYEE NAMES:** 1. 2. 3.	**EMPLOYEE NAMES:** 1. 2. 3.
			• What's impeding their performance? • Change role/manager? • Coach – performance manage*; offboard if no improvement	• Challenge – provide leadership and stretch assignments • Provide a mentor • Reward and engage	• Provide special development opportunities • Reward and recognize • Challenge and engage

		4. UNDER-PERFORMER	5. KEY PLAYER	6. CURRENT STAR
POTENTIAL	EVOLVING POTENTIAL	• Underperformer • Obstacles to performance? • Questionable fit	• Achieves goals • Some potential for growth • Needs greater challenges	• Exceeds targets • Valued contributor • Potential for growth
		EMPLOYEE NAMES: 1. 2. 3.	**EMPLOYEE NAMES:** 1. 2. 3.	**EMPLOYEE NAMES:** 1. 2. 3.
		• What's impeding their performance? • Challenge them • Coach – performance manage*; offboard if no improvement	• Provide coaching and development opportunities • Provide stretch assignments	• Actively develop for next level • Provide a mentor • Provide development and growth opportunities
	REACHED POTENTIAL	**1. MARGINAL** • Underperformer • Unlikely to improve	**2. SOLID PERFORMER** • Achieves goals • Steady contributor • Content with status quo	**3. FUNCTIONAL EXPERT** • Exceeds targets • Loves job • Content with status quo
		EMPLOYEE NAMES: 1. 2. 3.	**EMPLOYEE NAMES:** 1. 2. 3.	**EMPLOYEE NAMES:** 1. 2. 3.

POTENTIAL	REACHED POTENTIAL	• Performance manage*; offboard if no improvement	• Motivate and engage • Discuss their future goals • Provide resources for consistent performance	• Engage, challenge and reward • Discuss their future goals • Can mentor others, share their knowledge
		LOW Unacceptable	AVERAGE Meets expectations	HIGH Exceeds expectations
	PERFORMANCE			

Tool 2.3: Employee Career Development Checklist

As an employee, you are responsible for driving your own career. How effective are you at doing this?

How would your team members respond to these questions?

For career development enhancement, do you:

☐ Hold yourself accountable and ensure effective performance in your current role? (As an employee, it's essential that you are achieving your goals, and demonstrating that you are committed to your department and the organization.)

☐ Prioritize your own career development and regularly speak to your manager about your aspirations and career goals?

☐ Know your own skills and abilities, and how to best apply them?

☐ Know your values and passions and how they align with your organization's mission?

☐ Know your own value?
  ○ What are you uniquely contributing to your team/your organization?
  ○ Do others agree with this assessment?
  ○ Get feedback from your colleagues/stakeholders so you know how others perceive your contribution.

☐ Have a career development plan? (Assess yourself to determine the gap between where you are now – in terms of experience, skills and abilities – and where you want to be in the future, so you can speak to your leader about how to close the gap. See Tools 2.4 and 2.5 – Career Development Action Plan and Instructions).

☐ Take advantage of any educational, learning or growth opportunities offered by your organization?

☐ Ensure there is an alignment between your personal goals and those of the organization? (The more closely they are matched, the more effective, productive and engaged you will be.)

☐ Ensure that you and your colleagues learn from each other?

☐ Develop relationships at work so you are well-connected?

☐ Make it a priority to be helpful to others?

☐ Have a mentor?

Tool 2.4: Career Development Action Plan Instructions

This tool will be especially helpful for those of you who work at organizations that don't have their own career development process.

The goal of this activity is to develop your vision for your career over the next few years. Where do you want to be five years from now?

You can use this information in your career planning discussions with your manager.

Step 1: Your Target Vision – List your career goals.

Vision – How do you envision your career path over the next one, three, five, and ten years? Do not limit yourself to your current career. There may be other leadership or career goals you want to achieve, such as starting your own company, helping to create a new non-profit organization, or getting into politics. This vision will help you to decide where you want to invest your time and energy so that you will achieve the results you want.

Imagine it is five years into the future and you are thinking back on your career accomplishments over the last five years. What are these accomplishments? If you do not set your target, you will not know where you are going, or when and if you get there!

Write down your career vision:

Step 2: Required Competency List – List the required competencies for each goal. See table 1 (page 3) column B for an example.

In order to accomplish your five-year vision, what are the skills, abilities, and knowledge a person in this position would need? This list makes up the required set of competencies a successful person in this career would possess. You may need to do some research to find out what the necessary skills and competencies are for each goal.

Step 3: Analysis of Current Competencies – Assess your current abilities. See table 1, column C for an example.

Take a look at the list of competencies and assess your current ability on each competency: is it fully developed or does it need further development? You may be surprised to find you have some fully developed competencies already – great! This plan is to assist you in your own development, so make sure you are honest and realistic both in terms of your evaluation of your current skills and in terms of how much you will be able to accomplish each year. Remember, you have a personal life, too! Keeping these things in mind will result in an inventory of the competencies in which you are already proficient as well as a list of those competencies which need further development i.e. your strengths and opportunities for growth.

The result is your gap analysis. The gap is the difference between your future vision or your target and where you are now.

Step 4: Create an Action Plan

From this gap analysis, you can create your action plan to ensure you will reach your target in the time frame you have set. For this action plan, write your short term one- to two-year and longer term three- to five-year goals. In describing how these goals will be achieved, create an action plan. Create a reasonable timeline for accomplishing the goals in your action plan. Determine the action steps in your plan, how you will achieve them, and by when. Address the following questions:

- How are you going to close the gap to ensure you acquire the necessary skills, abilities and knowledge?
- What specific actions will you have to take to make it happen?
- What kinds of training, education, and other experiences are necessary?
- What will you have to do to acquire the under-developed skills and abilities which are needed to achieve your goals?

Consider opportunities available at work. Here are a few ideas; keep in mind, not all of them will be applicable or possible for you:

- Ask your manager for coaching regarding a specific area.
- Ask your manager for specific assignments in the areas of interest (including stretch assignments). How can you add value to the organization?
- What job-crafting opportunities are available?
- Ask for a transfer to a different department.
- Volunteer for special assignments, taskforces, or committees.
- Utilize the training opportunities which are offered at work.
- Find a mentor.
- Become a mentor.
- Network with others in your organization.

Consider opportunities available outside of work:

- Training courses/seminars.
- Adult education classes.
- Other kinds of experiences which might assist you through management or committee experience such as joining your Home Owners' Association, the Parent Teachers Association, or a non-profit organization.
- Volunteer to coach a team.
- Join a professional organization.
- Make a presentation at a conference, or at a professional organization meeting.
- Write articles about your areas of interest.
- Network with others in your field/in the area in which you want to progress.
  - How about going on some informational interviews in companies you like and with people who would be able

to give you information about the kind of work in which you are interested?

- At the end of the interview, don't forget to ask for the names of a couple of other people who would also be willing to talk to you.

Here are a couple of additional things to consider:

- Remember that your goals should be SMART: specific, measurable, achievable, realistic, and timed or timely.
- Be realistic in terms of <u>what</u> you can achieve and <u>by when</u>. If you're studying, too, there is often not much time for anything else besides family.
- How will you know you are reaching your target?
- What is your timeline, and how will you monitor, measure, and evaluate your progress?

You ought to review your plan frequently, maybe once per month or, at least, once a quarter. You can also revise it when necessary to check off the items you have completed and to amend the action plan items as you re-prioritize your goals and amend your target.

As you develop your plan, it might be a good idea to put yourself in the place of a manager or mentor. If you were the mentor or supervisor of this person, what might be some recommendations you would suggest?

Table 1: Gap Analysis

A	B	C
Goals	**Required Competencies/ Experience**	**Fully Developed? (Y/N)***
Project management experience	Ability to lead meetings with all stakeholders	Y
"	Effective communication skills	N
"	Budgeting	Y
"	Time management	N
Facilitation skills	PowerPoint	N

* If not fully developed, see action plan.

From the information on this table, create your action plan—identify concrete action steps and a timeline; then state how you will measure/evaluate your progress.

Gap Analysis

A	B	C
Goals	**Required Competencies/ Experience**	**Fully Developed? (Y/N)***

* If not fully developed, see action plan.

Tool 2.5: Career Development Action Plan

Five-Year Goal:

#	COMPETENCY / EXPERIENCE	TASKS / ACTION STEPS	RESOURCES	TIME-LINE/ SUCCESS
1				
2				
3				
4				

Tool 2.6: Checklist for the Organization – Elements of Successful Career Development Programs

Successful Career Development Programs have the following features:

Culture and Commitment:

☐ The career development system has the commitment and support of top executives, demonstrated by financial and people resources (e.g., mentors).

☐ There is transparent and open communication of the company's career management philosophy.

☐ The organizational culture values and rewards learning and development.

Formal Talent Management Processes:

☐ The program includes an effective promotional process whereby employees who are promoted to managerial positions have the skills to be successful leaders. (The selection process is based on leadership skills and abilities, rather than on tenure or as a reward.)

☐ The organization has a formal succession planning program.

☐ Individual learning accounts are provided. (Each employee is given a certain amount of money to spend on work-related development.)

☐ There is continuous evaluation of the career development program:

- ○ Measuring return on investment for their career-development initiatives.
- ○ Surveys with employees to determine their satisfaction with the program.
- ○ A question during the "stay interview" about how satisfied the employee is with their career opportunities at the organization. (In "stay interviews," current employees are asked what they like and don't like about their position and why they remain in the organization. This gives managers/the organization feedback regarding how they can improve engagement and thus retain their valued employees.)
- ○ A question during the exit interview about how the employee felt about their career opportunities at the organization.

Manager Training/Accountability:
- ☐ Training is provided to leaders about the career development program, coaching, performance management, etc., so career conversations are of higher quality.
- ☐ Managers know how to create developmental opportunities/ stretch assignments for employees.
- ☐ There is the formalization of career development discussions with managers.
- ☐ Leaders/supervisors are held accountable for employee progress and are evaluated and rewarded on the growth and development of their direct reports.

Development Opportunities for Employees
- ☐ The career development program focuses on educating employees about their strengths and how to build on them (rather than focusing on weaknesses).

☐ The organization offers a wide range of development opportunities:

  ○ Workshops, online learning, seminars, conferences, mentoring/coaching, etc.

  ○ Experiential learning is highlighted (on-the-job training, projects, job rotation, special assignments, shadowing, etc.).

  ○ Learning and development opportunities are provided in various formats/technologies – accessible content, online learning, mobile learning, self-paced learning. (This is especially critical for Millennials.)

☐ There is the chance to learn from others in the organization:

  ○ Panel discussions, especially with leaders who have moved laterally to achieve their success.

  ○ Employee career centers / career fairs / job and talent banks.

  ○ Networking opportunities, e.g., a network of internal information providers

  ○ Mentoring / internal sponsor programs.

Chapter 3

Leverage Employee Strengths to Optimize Performance

. . . .

"A person can perform only from strength.
One cannot build performance on weaknesses,
let alone on something one cannot do at all"
–Peter Drucker

. . . .

Currently, there is a major explosion of "strengths" – strengths-based leadership, strengths-based coaching, strengths-based therapy, etc. A strength is a "consistent near perfect performance in an activity"[1] and stems from a person's innate talent, shaped by the combination of instinctive thought patterns and behaviors as well as knowledge and skills. A strength can also be viewed as "a pre-existing capacity for a particular way of behaving, thinking or feeling that is authentic, energising to the user, and enables optimal functioning, development and performance."[2] So, a strength is something that we find naturally effortless to do – so much so that we sometimes don't consider that behavior/skill a strength; we think that everyone finds it as easy as we do.

Before we begin our discussion, take a moment to assess your ability to leverage your employee's strengths by completing the survey below, using the scale:

Never (N), Rarely (R), Sometimes (S), Often (O) and Always (A)

At the bottom of the table, total the number of times you circle each letter. Consider your pattern:

- Which behaviors are you often or always doing? These indicate areas of strength for you.
- Which behaviors are you never or rarely doing? These suggest behaviors that you should try to do more frequently.

Rating	Strengths Focus
N R S O A	1. I know my team members' strengths.
N R S O A	2. I ensure that my team members know their own strengths.
N R S O A	3. I help my team members set weekly goals based on their strengths.
N R S O A	4. I encourage my team members to learn about each other's strengths.
N R S O A	5. In one-on-one meetings, I focus the discussion on my team member's strengths.
N R S O A	6. I match job roles/responsibilities with the strengths of each team member.

N R S O A	7. I leverage my team members' strengths at work.

The strengths movement has been around for a while; it was popularized in 2001 by Marcus Buckingham and Donald Clifton in their book "Now, Discover Your Strengths."[1] (Buckingham used to work at The Gallup Organization and Clifton is "the father of strengths psychology"). In their book, they stated that they wanted to start a strengths revolution – and they did! They describe the thirty-four themes (talents) of the CliftonStrengths (formerly the StrengthsFinder) assessment and suggest ideas for managing strengths and creating a strengths-based company.

The strengths focus is strongly informed by positive psychology and appreciative inquiry. Rather than focusing on a person's weaknesses and what they did "wrong," positive psychology focuses on cultivating a person's strengths – their talents and skills, what they're good at – and what they do "right." What is working well? What motivates, inspires and gives hope? What are the root causes of success? This approach is a major paradigm shift; rather than spending time and energy trying to shore up weaknesses, managers focus on harnessing their employees' – and their team's – strengths, successes and achievements. Nurturing and using strengths builds resilience, relieves stress and promotes engagement and "being in the flow."

Case Example – Mervyn Davies (now Lord Davies)[3]

Mervyn Davies joined the Standard Chartered Bank in 1997 and held several executive positions during the ten years he was there – his last position as chairman. He helped to turn the bank around, making it one of the most respected banks in London.[4] Davies was an early believer in the strengths-based approach. He used his strength for learning to continuously improve himself (during his first few years at the bank, he was stationed in Asia and learned to appreciate the cultures of the different countries). He had robust relationship-building skills. He spent time getting to know his executive team, identifying their strengths and weaknesses to determine best fit on the various teams. He was open with his employees, sharing some family challenges – his wife had breast cancer, and he emailed 400 top executives to let them know of the situation and that he'd be changing his schedule over the next few months. His openness and vulnerability thus allowed other staff members to put their families first too.[5] He used his ability to inspire others to motivate his executive team and the bank employees to achieve challenging goals – so much so that his bank weathered the economic downturn better than most others.

- - -

"Know yourself – your strengths and your weaknesses, so you can compensate in your teams for what you lack"
–Mervyn Davies

- - -

Relationship Between Employee Engagement and Strengths

The strengths movement has gained momentum as research repeatedly demonstrates the pivotal role a strengths focus plays in employee engagement. Gallup is one of the leading organizations in this field; they conduct a great deal of research and are involved in many consulting assignments in organizations to assess employee engagement, and then they facilitate interventions to improve engagement scores. They have been tracking employee engagement in the United States for over thirty years. Gallup has a series of twelve questions (Q12), which comprise their basic employee engagement survey questions. One of these Q12 questions focuses on whether an employee has an opportunity, every day, to work with her strengths.

People generally experience greater enjoyment at work and are more passionate about the tasks/projects in which they can utilize their strengths. Strengths usage frequently places people in a state of "flow", which means they lose track of time, are completely absorbed, and feel completely at one with what they're doing.[6] Who doesn't want to be so absorbed that you look at your watch, it's 2 p.m., and you just realized that you haven't eaten lunch yet!

Much research demonstrates the relationship between a strengths focus and employee engagement. There are two aspects to this – whether the employee can use their strengths at work on a daily basis, and whether or not managers focus on employee strengths during discussions. Each issue is discussed below:

- **Using Strengths at Work**: According to Rath and Conchie,[7] when an organization concentrates on its employees' strengths, the level of engagement can be as high as 73%

(versus a level of 9% in those organizations that don't focus on employee strengths). Positive Psychology research determined that people are happiest and most productive when they are using their signature character strengths. [8] In their research, the Corporate Leadership Council examined 106 performance-management strategies, and categorized these "drivers" according to their potential to increase employee performance.[9] They found that one of the top ("A-level") drivers –that have the potential to increase employee performance by 25% or more – is the opportunity to work on what the employee does best. This strategy was ranked at #7 out of 106: when employees are able to use their strengths at work, they are highly motivated and productive. A 2017 report indicated that 60% of respondents agreed that it is "very important" to be able to do what they do best in their job. In fact, all generations and genders placed the highest importance on this facet of work. Moreover, 54% of Millennials agreed that it was very important that they were able to use their talents at work.[10] Other research studies confirm the relationship between engagement and the daily use of strengths.[11]

- **Manager Focus**: There is a strong correlation between engagement and whether a manager focuses on employee strengths. When employees responded "strongly agree" to the statement "My manager focuses on my strengths or positive characteristics," 67% of them were engaged and only 2% were actively disengaged. On the other hand, when they answered "strongly disagree" to this statement, only 2% were engaged and 71% were actively disengaged.[12] In another study of Millennials, 70% said they were engaged when their managers focused on positive characteristics or their strengths, while only 39% were engaged when their managers focused on negative characteristics or weaknesses.[13]

So it's undeniable – using strengths every day results in higher engagement. As indicated above, there is also much higher engagement when a manager focuses on strengths and positive characteristics rather than weaknesses. Currently, on average, only 33% of workers in the USA are engaged, so why wouldn't you focus on the strengths of your direct reports (rather than their weaknesses) so you can double the number of employees who are engaged? Why wouldn't you ensure that your team members get to use their strengths every day? This seems to be an obvious way to lead as attention to strengths results in greater satisfaction, increased motivation, higher employee engagement and enhanced well-being.

What About Our Weaknesses?

With all this discussion about focusing on strengths – what about our weaknesses? Currently, many of us tend to focus on our weaknesses (and those of others!) as we have a natural negativity bias. For example, we concentrate more on the lower assessments of our performance at our annual review (even if we have five "Excellent" ratings, we – and our manager – focus on the one "Above Average" or "Average" rating). In reviewing those evaluations after a presentation, we concern ourselves more with the average or below average ratings, rather than ensuring that we make a note of the above average ratings, so that we can repeat those successes in the future and become even more effective with our presentations. If our child brings home a report card with four "A's", two "B's" and a "C," we concentrate on the "C" and get a tutor for our child. You get the picture …

Obviously, we can't ignore our weaknesses, but we can manage around them. A weakness is "anything that gets in the way of excellent performance." [1] Here are some ways to manage around them: [1] [14]

- Perhaps the weakness is a knowledge or skills gap, in which case training may help in overcoming the weakness – you can become good enough to get by. It may be as simple as creating a checklist so that you remember all the tasks involved in the process. Practicing the task may also help.
- If the weakness is in an area in which you have no talent, create a support system. This can be a person who has complementary strengths to you; you can partner together and help each other out – you fill in for each other's weaknesses. This is especially effective on a team when different team members can bring their strengths to the party and allow each person to focus on the tasks that are in their areas of strength.
- If you are able to, outsource your weakness – delegate that specific task.

Case Example – Warren Buffett Delegating

An example of this is the story of Warren Buffett giving away $31 billion to the Bill and Melinda Gates Foundation. People were surprised that he would allow other people to manage his philanthropic bequest. His reasons? First, the Gates' Foundation was already established, energized and demonstrating success with its initiatives. He thought they could distribute the money more effectively than he could. His second reason was that he didn't really enjoy philanthropy – he much preferred running his business – a strength of his. "And what I really want to do is keep doing what I enjoy doing."[15] Thus, he was able to outsource a weakness/what he didn't like to do so he could focus on an area of strength – on something he loved doing and in which he was highly skilled – managing his own business.[16]

- Drop it! Where possible, stop doing the activities that are weaknesses for you – redefine your role so the weakness is eliminated. How can you craft your job tasks so you can focus more on your areas of strength? (See Tool 1.2 – Job Crafting – in Chapter 1 for more information on this.)
- Leverage one of your strengths to overcome the weakness. As an example, suppose one of your weaknesses is networking. You're shy and don't feel confident in those "cocktail-party" situations, so you avoid networking both at work and at those monthly meetings of your professional organization. By avoiding networking, you're missing out on building valuable relationships and on hearing about important opportunities. You might have a strength of thoughtfulness or responsibility or being of service to others, and you could use any of these strengths to help you be more confident at those monthly meetings. You could decide that you're going to help the newer people by being on the "welcoming committee." In this role, you could make the newbies feel comfortable, give them the "lay of the land," introduce them to others, etc. As you use your strength, you won't be focusing on your shyness, but on being of service to the new members. Meanwhile you'll be building your network and feeling more confident at those meetings, thus, using your

strength of responsibility or thoughtfulness or service to help you overcome your networking weakness.

Strengths-Focused Mindset

• •

"It takes far less energy to move from first-rate performance to excellence than it does to move from incompetence to mediocrity."
—Peter Drucker

• •

A strengths-focused mindset has certain basic assumptions:

- Each employee has a unique set of strengths.
- Each person's greatest capacity for growth is in the areas of their natural talent, as people can leverage their strengths more easily than their weaknesses.1 According to Jim Clifton, "weaknesses never develop into strengths, while strengths develop infinitely" (see the "Deeper Dive" below for an illustration of this). In fact, if we focus on the areas we're not very good at – even if we put in lots of time and effort – we'll probably just come up to "average" (if we're lucky!). That's one of the problems with most performance appraisal systems – there is a keen focus on "developmental opportunities," which results in employees concentrating on their areas of weakness rather than on their strengths. By spending our time and effort trying to improve our weaknesses – rather than spending that time and effort in enhancing our strengths – we become mediocre in the areas of our weaknesses and stay at "above average" – instead of "excellent" – in our areas of strength.

DEEPER DIVE[17]

(For those who are interested in learning about a significant milestone in the strengths movement)

During the 1950s, the Nebraska School Study Council – in conjunction with the University of Nebraska – decided to support a project to research methods for teaching rapid reading. Participants were 10th graders (about 6,000 of them). They were from 2 groups, the "normal" and "gifted" students. The normal students could read (with comprehension) 90 words-per-minute (WPM), and the gifted students already read at a speed of 350 WPM (with comprehension). All the students were put through the same reading course, they practiced and had coaching. The results were that the normal group boosted their reading speed to 150 WPM – an increase of 66%. However, the gifted group boosted their reading speed to an astounding 2,900 WPM – a whopping 828% increase!

Donald Clifton was involved in this research – perhaps this was his first inkling that people could make their greatest improvements when they focused on their strengths.

* * *

"Weaknesses never develop into strengths, while strengths develop infinitely"
–Jim Clifton

Strengths-Based Organizations

Strengths-based organizations drive business results by leveraging the talent of their employees and teams. Strengths-based cultures have very little active disengagement.[18] However, the rationale for creating a strengths-based organization isn't just to improve employee engagement – it's also to enhance other areas of company performance. A meta-analysis found that by employing strengths-based interventions, organizations had increased sales, increased profits, higher employee engagement, higher customer engagement, and lower employee turnover. The percentages of the increases/decrease depended on the intensity of the intervention, which varied from merely making employees aware of their talents to advanced coaching and training for managers around their strengths.[19]

Besides the two assumptions mentioned above in a strengths-focused mindset, there are several essential strategies in a successful strengths-based organization:[20]

Employees Learn Their Own Strengths

Do your employees know their strengths (and do you know yours)? Tool 3.1 lists some resources to help with strengths identification. In addition, Tool 3.2 (Employee Checklist) has questions to prompt your employees to examine how to maximize the use of their strengths; you can also use this for yourself.

Reflection:

Think about a situation in the past, when you were recognized for a strength.

- *What are the details of the event?*
- *How did you feel?*
- *Did the use of your strength, and recognition of it, motivate and engage you?*
- *Did you determine to use that strength even more? How?*

Match Employee Strengths to Their Roles

Tool 3.3 (Strengths Profiles) provides questions so you can create strengths profiles for your team members, yourself and your boss. This will help you examine the strengths of your key collaborators so you can determine how to maximize their strengths usage in current and future projects.

Because you, as the departmental leader, know the skill sets of your staff, the various job roles, and which strengths are needed for each job task/project, you can determine the best fit of employee and responsibility. Even better, ask your team members to volunteer for the various assignments. They're going to select responsibilities that they enjoy doing and that align with their strengths, and they'll be more committed and energized as they've chosen the tasks themselves. See the case example at the end of the "Strengths-Based Teams" section for an illustration of this.

For team projects, you can ensure there is a diversity of strengths on each team. Thus, your employees can flourish as they are playing to their strengths and also developing as they gain experience and have the opportunity to try out new job tasks. In this way you are positioning your team members for success.

Employees Set Weekly Goals Based on Their Strengths

During your weekly meetings with your employees, encourage them to set weekly goals based on their strengths. How can they best meet expectations using their skills and talents? Which strength can they use as they set a stretch goal for themselves?

Provide Ongoing Coaching

It is important that team members realize they are becoming more effective and successful when they use their strengths. You can address this during your regular meetings with your employees. Point out when they've contributed to departmental success by using one of their strengths. See Tool 3.4 (Manager Checklist – Maximizing the Strengths of your Employees) for strategies to maximize your employees' strengths.

Coaching Around Strengths

Do you have the ability to coach your direct reports about their strengths? See Chapter 4 for more in-depth coverage on coaching. Here is some information specifically pertaining to coaching around strengths.

- One statistic showed that employees who received coaching on their strengths were 7.8% more productive than those who didn't receive the coaching.[21] Other researchers found that a coaching discussion which included debriefing a strengths report resulted in the employee having a better understanding of their strengths and being more likely to use them.[22] This points to the necessity for employees and their leaders to focus on strategies to ensure that the team member is using his strengths on the job to the greatest extent possible. As well as knowing what their strengths are, employees need to know how to use them. You can help your employees channel and prioritize their strengths. Which strength/s will they be using today? On which projects? How?

- Would you like to have at least 61% of your employees jumping out of bed in the morning to get to work? All it takes is a meaningful discussion with your employees about their strengths, so they feel appreciated and know that what they do is making an impact.[23]

Another aspect of coaching your employees is to help them <u>calibrate their strengths</u>.

- *Calibrating Strengths:* Some researchers emphasize that it's not enough to simply identify and use a strength – the situational context should be considered too.[24] What is the impact of using your strength right now in this situation? What effect will it have on others?

- Linley talks about the "Golden Mean" – "the right strength, to the right amount, in the right way, at the right time."[25] What is your golden mean – the optimal amount of your strength usage – in any particular situation? Do you need to dial your strength usage up or down? Are you not using your strength enough (underplaying), or are you overplaying your strength (so that it really becomes a weakness)? It's important that we use our strength in the right context and at the appropriate intensity.

- Coach your employees around this issue:
  - □ Have them reflect on situations when they've underplayed or overplayed a strength.
  - □ Discuss how they could determine the intensity needed in different circumstances – what would the "Golden Mean" look like?
  - □ Give them feedback about your observations of the intensity of their strength usage – when did they play their strength at the optimal intensity? If they under or overplayed, how could/should they have calibrated differently?

Case Example – Coaching A Client About Strength Calibration

One of us had a coaching client who had a strength in leading – particularly in urgent situations (e.g., if a key staff member was ill or suddenly quit during a significantly high-pressure situation or if someone had dropped the ball just before an important event). She immediately knew what to do to address the situation, and would direct her staff: "Jim, call X." "Maria, find out if we can …," Sally go down to Y department and …". Thus, she could resolve the issue/s, with the help of her staff and "save the day."

The problem arose when she had a similar dogmatic demeanor during meetings, saying things like "We should …" This created tension as she was perceived as being too authoritarian. When we discussed this during our coaching sessions, she realized that her "come, let's get this done" attitude worked well in crisis situations, but not necessarily at other times, such as during meetings. She realized she had to dial down her directing by first listening to others, asking for their input, and then making more tentative suggestions – "How about if we …," "What do you think about …?" Her colleagues and staff were much more open when she eased back in this manner. She also recognized that with her team members – when an urgent situation arose– rather than directing them, it was a teachable moment, one in which she could give her employees the opportunity to solve the problem themselves.

She had learned to adjust the intensity of her "leading" strength, depending on the circumstances. The subsequent 360° feedback score she received in this area of behavior (from colleagues, direct reports and manager) improved markedly.

Refer to Tool 3.4 (Manager Checklist – Maximizing the Strengths of your Employees) which has some more tactics to coach your team members around strengths usage.

Employees Learn the Strengths of Their Colleagues

Employees learn the strengths of their colleagues. Team members can work together most effectively if they are aware of each other's strengths. Do your direct reports know each other's strengths?

Strengths-Based Teams

Teams are more effective when they are created based on the strengths of the team members.[26] Each team member can do what they do best, what they enjoy doing, and because other team members have different—complementary—strengths, they can step in where there is less strength. If there are several responsibilities for a particular team project e.g., consolidating reports, facilitating training sessions and drumming up support, then ensuring the people tasked with those responsibilities are strong in those areas is vital. If one person enjoys networking and influencing people, they will be more effective in obtaining support; if another is very structured and loves analyzing facts, they will probably enjoy the reports piece; if someone else likes presenting they would probably prefer to facilitate the training. It wouldn't make sense to distribute the responsibilities in a different way – why would you task the networker with consolidating the reports if the networker isn't strong in report writing (and another team member is)? The networker won't be motivated working on the reports and probably won't be as effective as their more data-driven colleague.

Team members benefit from knowing the strengths of their colleagues. Successful teams focus on results and how the strengths of each person contribute to team productivity and organizational goals. Team members can see how each person is valuable to the team and ascertain the subject for which each individual would be the "go to" person. Teams that frequently focus on their strengths have 12.5% higher productivity and faster success.[27] These teams are more committed, collaborative and effective. Through team strength training, members learn to value and channel individual strengths, identify team shortfalls, and understand how this affects team performance. [28]

Only 39% of Millennials strongly agree that they know the strengths of their teammates (versus 46% of Non-Millennials).[13] What can you do to improve these figures? Here are some ways your team members (both Millennials and Non-Millennials) can get to know each other's strengths:

- Have your team members identify their own strengths (see Tool 3.1 – Resources for Identifying Strengths), then facilitate a meeting where everyone reveals their strengths, and the team discusses how their strengths can most effectively be utilized on their current projects/initiatives.
- When you are discussing a new/upcoming project, have the team talk about which employee would be most suited (based on their strengths) for each piece of the project.
- At your regular meetings, focus on one employee – ask the employee to name one strength and talk about how he has used it/is using it. The other team members can chime in and give feedback about when they've noticed their colleague demonstrating that particular skill and when that strength was used in support of the person giving feedback.
- You could start off your regular meetings acknowledging how you observed a team member using a particular strength in pursuit of a departmental goal. You could then ask employees to "shout out" colleagues, thanking them for how one of their strengths helped improve performance.
- Encourage team members to give feedback – in the moment – when they notice a colleague's strength contributing to success.

Case Example – A Strengths-Based Team

In a previous position, one of the authors worked on a professional development team. The team members knew each other's strengths and there was a high degree of trust. Every month, the team would meet (without their director) to look at the calendar for the following month and discuss the scheduled workshops, new consulting opportunities and any up-coming projects and initiatives. Each person volunteered for a specific number of workshops based on their interest and availability.

The discussion of the consulting, projects and initiatives focused on the strengths of the team members, as well as their areas of interest. It invariably turned out that there were volunteers for virtually all of the opportunities. (Occasionally, someone would have to take on a gig that they didn't really like, or that didn't fully play to their strengths, but each person took a turn at doing that.) It also provided training opportunities for team members – if someone was newer or wanted to try out a different kind of task – and they didn't feel comfortable doing it on their own – they were teamed up with one of their colleagues so they could learn the process and meet the relevant people involved in the project.

Team members could also propose their own projects/initiatives.

It was a highly productive, committed and engaged team; certainly the best team experience of the author's career.

Tool 3.5 (Strengths Team Building Activity) describes a simple and fun teambuilding activity with a strengths' discussion debrief.

Everyone in the Organization is Committed

Leaders, employees, and the organization are committed to maintaining a strengths-based organization.

- You demonstrate your commitment to your employees' strengths-based development during your regular feedback meetings with your staff.
- Employees recognize that their peers are committed when team members work well together and offer each other feedback on strengths usage.
- The organization validates its commitment by:
  - Executive buy-in and support, demonstrating that the organization is committed to developing the strengths of each individual.
  - Awareness – there is company-wide awareness, with all employees sharing a common strengths language.
  - There is a network of strengths champions.
  - Alignment – all HR/management processes (recruiting, onboarding, employee development, performance management, promotions, succession planning and off-boarding) are aligned and strengths-based.

Case Example – Triad Group [29]

In 2014, because of several leadership changes and poor communication with production teams, one of the Triad Group subsidiaries had extremely high employee turnover (85% per month!) and high defect rates. The owners decided that they would turn the company around by changing the culture of the organization to a strengths-based one. All employees took a strengths assessment and participated in a six-week training and coaching program, which focused on understanding strengths and how to leverage them on teams. Employees were given strengths calendars (so they could concentrate on their strengths daily) and jerseys (which had their top talent printed on the back). On Fridays everyone wore their jerseys to work.

To enhance team cohesion and display the diversity of strengths, team strength grids were posted on the shop walls. Each shift change starts with a meeting that focuses on how the employees' strengths can be used to handle that day's work. In an effort to create/sustain this new strengths-based organizational culture and thus improve productivity and employee engagement, other interventions were employed. (The management team attended a "High Performance Management" course, an employee engagement survey was administered, and initiatives were implemented based on the results).

The outcomes were spectacular – within two years, monthly turnover fell from 85% to 8%, defect rates dropped from 35% to 1%, productivity increased by 200% and profitability increased by 233% – all with the same number of employees.

This demonstrates the powerful impact of a strengths-based organization on company performance.

Building a strengths-based and engaging organization entails effort and commitment from employees and leaders alike. Are you inspiring your employees to play to their strengths so everyone can win at work? Even though your organization may not be trying to change its culture to become strengths-based, you can still become a strengths-based department by championing strengths and introducing some strengths initiatives in the areas under your control. Can you become a strengths champion and encourage your colleagues to join the strengths movement? If it isn't already, how can you influence your company to become a strengths-based organization? See Tool 3.6 – Elements of Strengths-Based Organizations, for strategies to create and maintain a strengths-based organization.

Takeaways

- Strengths-based organizations have increased sales, higher profits, lower turnover and higher employee and customer engagement.
- There is a very high correlation between employee engagement and an emphasis on workers' strengths.
- There are several strategies to handle our weaknesses:
  □ Get trained and practice
  □ Create a support system
  □ Delegate it
  □ Drop it
  □ Use a strength to overcome the weakness.
- A strengths-focused mindset assumes each person has a unique set of strengths and their greatest capacity for growth is in their areas of strength.
- Ensure each of your employees know their own strengths.
- Coaching employees regarding their strengths results in higher productivity.

- Strengths usage is contextual and the intensity needs to be calibrated.
- Ensure there's a "best fit" between employee strengths and their goals/tasks.
- Ensure your team members know each other's strengths.
- Have team members split their roles/responsibilities based on their strengths.
- Focus on strengths-based employee development.

A strengths focus seems such a simple thing to do, and the results are so positive – higher satisfaction and motivation, improved productivity, enhanced well-being, etc. – and yet this is a tool that some managers and organizations don't utilize. We recommend that you review the checklists below, to ensure you are inspiring yourself and your team members to higher levels of engagement through the utilization of their strengths.

Tool 3.1: Resources for Identifying Strengths

A. There are commercially available tools for identifying strengths. The two that are most prominent are the CliftonStrengths (formerly known as StrengthsFinder) and the VIA Character Survey.

CliftonStrengths: This 177-item assessment is a web-based instrument that helps individuals identify their strengths across thirty-four themes or domains. The survey can be taken for a fee at: www.gallupstrengthscenter.com

VIA Survey of Character Strengths: This survey was created under the direction of Dr. Martin Seligman, known as the father of Positive Psychology, and Dr. Christopher Peterson. It has been scientifically validated and used in hundreds of research studies around the world. This survey features twenty-four character strengths. The survey can be taken for free at www.viacharacter.org

B. Alternatively, you can also reflect on your own individual strengths (or those of your team member) by answering the following questions:
- What are you good at (skills, competencies)?
- What makes you unique?
- What are you the "go to" person for?
- How would others describe your strengths?
- What do you most enjoy doing at work?
- What are you doing when you "get lost" in your tasks and time flies by?

- Recall past feedback (e.g., when praised, comments in performance reviews).
- Reflect on your life successes, both professional and personal, to identify which strengths led to your achievements.

C. Buckingham* suggests that one way of figuring out your strengths is to review your day (or keep a journal during the day). Put a line down the middle of the page, and title one side "Love it" and title the other side "Loathe it." In the appropriate column, write down the tasks you did during the day. On the "Love it" side will be the responsibilities that you enjoyed, that energized you and that put you "in the flow." On the "Loathe it" side will be the tasks that drained and de-energized you. As you review these lists, you'll probably find that you were working with your strengths during the tasks in the "Love it" column.

* Buckingham, M. (2015). StandOut 2.0: Assess your strengths, find your edge, win at work. Harvard Business Review Press.

Tool 3.2: Employee Checklist – Maximizing the Use of Your Strengths

Do you:

- [ ] Know your strengths?
  - ○ List your top five strengths
  - ○ How does each one help you perform effectively at work?
  - ○ How could you use a strength in a new way?
  - ○ Which one/s are underutilized?
  - ○ How could you increase their use at work?
- [ ] Examine how to harness these strengths effectively at work?
- [ ] Determine the activities during which you experience "being in the flow?"
- [ ] Figure out how to calibrate each strength, depending on the situation?
- [ ] Make sure you "do what you do best" at work, every day?
- [ ] Set weekly goals, based on your strengths?
- [ ] Review your weekly accomplishments; how has the utilization of your strengths facilitated your success?
- [ ] Request projects/job tasks that align with your strengths?
- [ ] Ensure you have regular meetings with your manager to discuss your strengths?
- [ ] Create a role that utilizes your strengths every day?
- [ ] Recraft your job responsibilities to match your strengths?
- [ ] Ask your team members (and boss) to tell you when they've seen you at your best/when they've seen you use your strengths?

☐ Get to know the strengths of your colleagues?

☐ Have discussions with your colleagues to determine how you can best work together using each other's strengths?

You are an employee too. Ensure you answer the questions in this section for yourself.

Tool 3.3: Strengths Profiles for Employees and Leaders

Create a strengths profile for your direct reports, yourself and your boss.

1. Examine the strengths of your direct reports – one page for each person
   - Name
   - Top five strengths/passions
   - Current projects – which strengths are being used?
   - How can you harness their strengths even further to accomplish their goals?
     - □ Which strengths are underutilized?
     - □ How could their use at work be increased?
   - Upcoming projects – what are the necessary skills/ strengths? With which projects is there a best fit with the employee's strengths?

2. Create a Strengths Profile for yourself – how can you nurture your own strengths?
   - List your top five strengths
   - How does each one help you perform effectively at work?
   - Which one/s are underutilized?
   - How could you increase their use at work?
   - Which upcoming projects/initiatives interest you most? How can you become involved in them?

3. How can you work more effectively with your boss?
   - What are your supervisor's top strengths?
   - How do your strengths complement theirs?
   - What are their weaknesses?
   - How can you step in with your strengths to support them?
   - Reviewing current and upcoming projects, how can you work most productively to make their life easier? (After all, isn't that what all bosses want?)

Tool 3.4: Manager Checklist – Maximizing the Strengths of your Employees

Do you maximize the strengths of your employees by:

- [ ] Ensuring your direct reports know their own strengths?
- [ ] Coaching your employees so they know how to maximize their strengths?
- [ ] Focusing on results, rather than being prescriptive regarding how to do the work? (In this way, the employee can decide on the most effective way of achieving the goal, in alignment with their strengths.)
- [ ] Reinforcing the significance of strengths use by asking an employee – towards the end of the day – a question such as:
  - ○ Today, have you been able to "do what you do best?"
  - ○ What have you most enjoyed about your work today?
  - ○ When have you been in the flow today?
  - ○ Which strength/s have you used today?
  - ○ Which parts of your job have you not liked today?
- [ ] Helping your employee calibrate their strengths? Ask them:
  - ○ Which strengths are you underplaying? How could you dial up the usage? In which situations would you do this?
  - ○ Which strengths are you overplaying? How could you dial down the usage? In which situations would you do this?
  - ○ My observations are …
- [ ] Focusing on how the diversity of team strengths are effective in achieving departmental goals?

☐ Having regular (at least quarterly) meetings with each employee focusing the coaching discussion on their strengths?
  ○ What are your strengths?
  ○ How could they be utilized even further?
  ○ How are they helping you be more effective and successful?
  ○ How do your strengths align with your goals?
  ○ When you use your strengths, here's the impact you have …
  ○ How do they align with the organization's goals?
  ○ Telling your employee the unique value they deliver to the department, to the company (the impact of their strengths use on their teammates, etc.)?

☐ Reflecting on how you could support your team members so they are "in the flow" more frequently?

☐ Ensuring your direct reports know the strengths of their colleagues?

☐ Reviewing the roles/activities of your employees and examining how you can allocate those job responsibilities based on the different talents of your team members?

☐ Helping your direct reports to recraft* their job responsibilities to match their strengths? (Job crafting was addressed in chapter 1. See Tool 1.2.)

☐ Frequently and publicly recognizing the strengths of your employees?

☐ Ensuring you include a strengths discussion during performance reviews?

☐ Examining where there are gaps in your strengths/experience for which some of your direct reports could step in? This will make your life easier and give them developmental opportunities.

☐ Determining how you could "create a community of strengths advocates and champions." *

---

* Sorenson, S. (2014). How employees' strengths make your company stronger. Retrieved from https://news.gallup.com/businessjournal/167462/employees-strengths-company-stronger.aspx.

Tool 3.5: Strengths Team Building Activity

The following describes a team-building activity for employees and leaders. This would follow an in-depth explanation and assessment of strengths (using any strengths tool). In this activity, participants will see how their strengths are utilized (or not utilized enough) in a group setting.

Materials:
- A stack of fifty index cards per group
- A roll of masking tape per group

Time: 45 minutes

Goal: To create the tallest tower using only the index cards and masking tape.

Directions:
1. Create groups in teams of four to seven people.
2. Discuss with the participants the goal of the activity and their supplies.
3. Groups will have fifteen minutes to complete the goal.

Tips:
- As the groups create their towers, give them periodic time warnings.
- When a winner is announced, keep spirits high by admiring all towers and quickly bring the groups together for debrief.

Debrief Questions:

- How did you come up with your tower? What did that process look like?
- What feelings did you experience? (Probing question: Tell me more…)
- How did it feel when your group members agreed with your ideas?
- How did it feel when they disagreed with your ideas?
- How were the strengths of different members shown in this exercise?
- Were some group member strengths not utilized in this exercise?
- Why do you think those strengths were not used?
- How could you (individual member) have utilized your strengths more?
- How could the team have utilized the strengths of each member more?
- How can you utilize the strengths you used here in your work roles?
- What have we learned about using strengths to engage employees and build stronger teams?

Contributed by: Roberto Bueno, Rachel Choate and Vivian Tu, Alliant International University

FYI, this is similar to another team-building exercise, the "Marshmallow Challenge." Details of this can be found through a Google search. Here is a TED talk on it: https://www.teachmeteamwork.com/teachmeteamwork/2010/08/build-a-tower-build-a-team-a-team-building-activity-by-tom-wujec.html#sthash.dlGjLnVw.dpuf.

Tool 3.6: Elements of Strengths-Based Organizations

Assumptions
- Each employee has a unique set of strengths.
- Each person's greatest capacity for growth is in the areas of their natural talent.

Strategies to Create and Maintain a Strengths-Based Organization

- Employees:
  - Learn their own strengths.
  - Learn the strengths of their colleagues.
  - Set weekly goals based on their strengths.
- Managers/Leaders:
  - Commit to strengths-based development.
  - Match the roles and responsibilities of each employee to their strengths.
  - Provide ongoing coaching about the connection between strengths usage and success and how to effectively calibrate strengths
  - Encourage employees to set weekly goals based on their strengths.
  - Ensure they have a quarterly meaningful strengths-focused career discussion with each employee (more on this in Chapter 4).
  - Create teams based on strengths.
- The organization is committed to:
  - Executive buy-in and support.

□ Company-wide awareness of strengths
□ Network of strengths champions
□ All HR and management processes are aligned and strengths-based.

You, as a manager, have a fair amount of control regarding the first two sections above.

- Would your employees agree to the statements in the first section?
- As an employee, what is your response?
- How would you respond to the statements in the second section?
- How could you champion a strengths-based perspective more fully?

The organizational features are less under your control.

- If your organization doesn't incorporate these features, maybe you can influence your organization to change its culture to become more strengths-based.
- How could you advocate for these organizational features??

Chapter 4

Use Performance Management to Engage Employees

"A company might have a world-class performance-management system in place, but the system is only as effective as the managers who implement it."
–Oberoi & Rajgarhia

In this chapter, we will be discussing how leaders can manage performance to engage their employees and teams. We'll first give a broader overview of the organization's talent-management perspective. As a manager, you don't necessarily have much authority over the strategic aspects of talent management; however, you have a great deal of control over how you manage the performance of your team members, which is the focus of this chapter.

Strategic Talent Management

An organization's strategic talent management system is an integrated process aimed at increasing productivity and achieving results by linking employee and organizational performance. This system's primary purpose is to ensure organizational goals are met through the maximization of employee effort, commitment and success. It includes the employee experience through the whole talent life cycle: recruiting, selection, onboarding, compensation, rewards and benefits, career development and termination.

Goals of a talent management system include:

- Effective recruitment and selection
- Optimization of employee talent
- Professional development support
- Performance measurement
- Evaluation, selection and assessment practices
- Equitable compensation/rewards
- Helping managers make pay and promotional decisions as well as demotion and termination decisions

All organizational practices should support the holistic talent management system, and all processes need to be aligned to generate the desired results. Feedback, coaching, tracking, behavioral data gathering and preparation for performance planning and review all require time, commitment and skill to make them work effectively.

Performance Management

Within this talent management system is the performance management process, which occurs between a manager and her direct reports. This is how leaders maximize the performance of their workers to achieve the organization's goals. Some people think the performance management process refers only to feedback given to the employee at the annual performance review. However, there is a difference between a performance appraisal – merely that annual meeting (which both manager and employee usually dislike so intensely) – and the continuous performance management relationship (a daily or weekly ongoing one) in which the annual or semi-annual meeting is merely a "re-view" (no surprises!). Continuous, effective performance management is essential, as it contributes to employee engagement, retention and optimal performance.[1]

Effective Performance Management means employees:

- Know their strengths (Chapter 3)
- Understand how their positions contribute to the success of the organization
- Know their performance expectations
- Are treated with respect and inclusion (Chapter 5)
- Are given the correct tools/training/coaching/resources necessary for effective performance
- Are recognized for good work
- Set development goals for themselves, in collaboration with their manager (Chapter 2)
- Understand their career path and growth opportunities (Chapter 2)
- Are rewarded fairly for work effort
- Hold themselves and their team-mates accountable (this chapter)

Reflection:

Review the list above. *Would your team members respond "yes" to these statements?*

Relationship Between Employee Engagement and Performance Management

• •

"I am no different than the average employee. If I had an understanding of what the organization needed, why the organization was doing what it was doing, and how my role and actions fit in, then I was super engaged."
–David Norton, former group chairman, Global Pharmaceuticals, Johnson & Johnson

• •

Research found that when managers were successful at performance management, their employees were more engaged, more productive and more creative than those who reported to managers who were ineffective performance leaders.[2] Performance planning, continuous feedback and coaching, and accountability are the critical pieces of effective performance management that result in employee engagement. We'll now address these crucial aspects of performance management in detail.

Performance Planning

Before reading further, assess your performance planning skills by completing the survey below, using the scale:

Never (N), Rarely (R), Sometimes (S), Often (O) and Always (A).

At the bottom of the table, total the number of times you circle each letter. Consider your pattern:

- Which behaviors are you often or always doing? These indicate areas of strength for you.
- Which behaviors are you never or rarely doing? These suggest behaviors that you should try to do more frequently.

Rating	Performance Planning
N R S O A	1. I make sure that my team members know what is expected of them.
N R S O A	2. I discuss how each team member's work aligns with the goals of the department and the organization.
N R S O A	3. I set goals collaboratively with my team members.
N R S O A	4. I ensure that my team members have the correct tools and resources for optimal work performance.

Even though it seems obvious, it is imperative that team members know – in detail – what is expected of them, how they are progressing towards those objectives, and how their work supports the department's and organization's goals. Researchers found that the top drivers of employee engagement included clarity around the company's priorities and receiving feedback on work performance.[3]

Engagement is promoted when managers help employees understand how their work aligns with the organization's strategy.[4] Researchers discovered that only 15% of employees knew what their organizations were trying to accomplish – 85% weren't sure![5] Another study revealed that employees were 3.5 times more likely to be engaged when they strongly agreed that they understood the linkage between their own and the organization's goals.[6] This illustrates how essential it is that the manager focuses on the organization's mission and objectives when setting goals with employees, and highlights how each team member's work impacts organizational results. Employees like to know how they make a difference to the business – how their effort and work support the company's mission and values.

In fact, 28% of the disengaged employees, when asked which element would most improve their performance, selected their first choice as "greater clarity about what the organization needs me to do, and why."[7] It is surprising that more than a quarter of disengaged employees don't have clarity around performance expectations. If they had this understanding, would that have moved them over into the "engaged" group? Probably not all, but perhaps some of them.

Goal Setting

Goal setting is at the core of performance management, and it is collaborative goal setting that drives employee engagement. When employees participate in creating their own goals, not only is there more buy-in on their part – but often the goals that are generated are more challenging than if the manager assigns the goals himself. In addition, the ensuing discussion around strategies to achieve the collaborative goal results in a dialogue that is developmental for the employees.[4] Collaborative goal setting motivates team members as they can focus on the parts of their work that engages them the most. Employees who strongly agree that they set goals collaboratively with their managers are nearly four times more likely to be engaged than other workers.[6]

A study found that specific behaviors determined whether managers were engaging or disengaging.[8] Except for these particular behaviors, engaging managers didn't have very much in common with each other – they varied in terms of experience, role, management training, etc. The engaging leaders were especially strong in clearly setting expectations, being results-focused and providing feedback.

These results were repeated in a more recent study, which found that 66% of employees who strongly agreed that their managers helped in setting priorities, and 69% who strongly agreed that their managers helped in setting performance goals, were engaged. Of the employees who were actively disengaged, 53% strongly disagreed with each of these statements.[2] Surprisingly, only 50% of employees fully understand what is expected of them at work.[6]

This demonstrates how leaders can increase engagement when they help in establishing a team member's priorities and goals. For the actively disengaged employees, how might their engagement levels be affected if their managers helped them to set goals and prioritize their work? These two aspects of management are so basic, and yet it seems that many leaders don't help their employees to set priorities and goals.

Reflection:

As a manager, how do you ensure your employees have clear performance expectations and agreements?

Continuous Feedback and Coaching

Before reading further, assess your feedback skills by completing the survey below, using the scale:

Never (N), Rarely (R), Sometimes (S), Often (O) and Always (A).

At the bottom of the table, total the number of times you circle each letter. Consider your pattern:

- Which behaviors are you often or always doing? These indicate areas of strength for you.
- Which behaviors are you never or rarely doing? These suggest behaviors that you should try to do more frequently.

Rating	Feedback Skills
N R S O A	1. I give frequent feedback.
N R S O A	2. I give feedback immediately.
N R S O A	3. I give specific and constructive feedback.
N R S O A	4. I recognize effective performance.
N R S O A	5. I recognize progress/improvement in performance.
N R S O A	6. I provide a system whereby team members can gauge their own progress.

The second component of performance management is continuous feedback and coaching. This includes regular feedback and the identification of training needs for employees (to build the competencies necessary for effective performance). An essential aspect of successful management is the ability to coach all staff – whether star performers or those whose performance is under par. Team members should be recognized and rewarded for the work they do and be held accountable when work is not up to standard. Additionally, managers need to be able to conduct an effective formal review discussion. In this section, we will be focusing on giving feedback and coaching.

Giving Feedback

Research shows that frequent, immediate feedback (e.g., regular touch points/check-ins) enhances performance and engagement.[9] Feedback should be specific, not personal, constructive, sincere, timely (done soon after the behavior), frequent, and recognize effective performance and/or progress.

In one study, when asked which item would most improve performance, 13% percent of the disengaged employees selected "Regular, specific feedback about how I'm doing" (as their third choice) and 21% of engaged employees also selected this item (as their second choice). So ... both disengaged and engaged employees stated that their performance would be improved with effective feedback.[1] Unfortunately, a survey of managers in the U.S. found that **only 2%** of managers provide ongoing feedback to their employees.[10] This is an astounding statistic! It seems that this essential piece of performance management is sorely lacking in the American workforce – 98% of managers don't provide continuous feedback to their direct reports. If feedback is such an important element – to both engaged and disengaged workers – why aren't more leaders doing it? Why are so many managers falling short on this essential aspect of their job?

Reflection:

Do you give ongoing, specific and timely feedback to your team members? If not, why not?

Effective managers ensure that goals are measurable and progress can be evaluated objectively. In this section, we're talking about "giving feedback." However, it's even more effective (and one of the reasons why technology solutions are recommended) when employees can gauge their own progress – i.e. receive feedback on their contribution without having to rely on their manager. Because Millennials are used to constant, on-going communication, that is what they want from their supervisors. Rather than waiting for an annual review, they want real-time, continuous feedback that is going to support them in their current work and future development.[11]

Tools and processes that make it easier to give ongoing feedback are essential – especially for Millennials. It is a good idea to schedule short check-ins and reviews with employees, and, if available, incorporate feedback apps, pulse surveys and anonymous social networking tools for immediate feedback. Remember too that informal feedback is an essential piece of the engaging manager's toolkit. Feedback can be in-person, by phone, text, instant messaging, email or videoconferencing.

Case Example –
Culture of Performance Feedback[12]

Over the last few years, Booz Allen streamlined its performance management system by eliminating ratings. The results of an annual company survey revealed that employees wanted more in-depth and frequent feedback about their performance and career possibilities. The company introduced a pilot program of SnapShot – a system that facilitated regular feedback conversations. Managers received training on conducting feedback and career discussions. They had monthly mandatory 10-15 minute discussions with each employee. For accountability and tracking, both manager and employee had to complete a short survey.

Six months after the introduction of the SnapShot pilot program, employee survey results indicated that through the monthly conversations, employees felt more supported, understood expectations more clearly, and had a better understanding of the organization's career development opportunities. Manager survey results revealed that they felt much more confident coaching their employees and felt their relationships with employees had improved.

Ninety-five percent of participants valued their feedback conversations and 80% of managers observed enhanced employee engagement.

Booz Allen is now implementing a company-wide launch of a feedback system.

Feedback is a two-way street. Do you ask your employees for feedback? One way of obtaining feedback is to conduct stay and exit interviews. You can use the information from exit interviews to ensure you continue positive strategies (e.g., the employee may have said that you were great at clarifying goals and expectations), and amend managerial behaviors that didn't work well (e. g, the employee stated that he felt micro-managed). "Stay" interviews improve engagement and retention. In Stay interviews, current employees are asked what they like and don't like about their position, if their expectations are being met and why they remain in the organization. This gives managers/the organization information regarding how they can improve engagement thus increasing the likelihood of retaining their valued employees.

Coaching for Success

• •

*"Coaching is an approach, not an event that needs
to be scheduled."*
–BlessingWhite

• •

In the previous section, we've discussed the crucial need for ongoing feedback. Yes, feedback is essential; however, when talking about performance management, how does feedback from a coaching perspective compare?

Which is most beneficial – constructive feedback or positive coaching? Buckingham and Goodall describe an experiment (conducted by Jack, Boyatzis and colleagues) in which participants were monitored to see which parts of the brain were stimulated during various kinds of conversations[13]. The researchers found that when people were given constructive feedback which focused on their shortcomings and what they needed to fix, they showed a fight or flight response. The feedback received about their limitations (even though it was "constructive") was perceived as a threat, invoking anxiety and sadness, effectively closing them down and reducing the possibility of learning.

On the other hand, when participants received positive coaching, their parasympathetic nervous system was activated – they felt a sense of well-being – an improved mood and a sense of more openness – a state in which it is easier to learn. Buckingham and Goodall suggest that we should concentrate on catching our employees when they have performed exceptionally well – when they've done something that amazed us! By highlighting the situation and helping the team member analyze her successful behaviors in this moment of excellence, she comes to learn and understand what "genius" looks like for her. Together you can thus explore the specific "nature of excellence" of each employee, coaching your team members on how they can repeat these outstanding behaviors in the future.

Compared to traditional feedback, coaching is a more empowering and collaborative process during which you both work together, focusing on enhancing performance.

What is the difference between traditional feedback and coaching?

Traditional Feedback	Coaching
Focus on past Can be directive Provide answers	Focus on future Collaborative Provide questions
Both	
Accountability Measure and track results Need to be trained to do it effectively Continuous Takes time and effort	

One of the main differences is that coaching involves asking, whereas feedback often focuses on telling. Here's an example of a scenario, which demonstrates the difference between feedback and coaching:

An employee is the project manager of a significant project, and she just held a meeting with important stakeholders. In giving her traditional feedback, her manager might say:

- "I noticed that when Jack challenged your idea about ....., you didn't stand up for yourself. It would have been better if, rather than backing down, you had calmly reiterated the results of the survey and waited to see how he responded to that – perhaps asking the other VPs for their thoughts."

However, the coaching conversation would be much different as the leader would ask questions such as:

- How did you feel when Jack challenged your idea about …?
- Are you satisfied with your response?
- What might you have done differently?
- What can you do to prepare for that kind of issue in the future?
- Is there anything you could do now to persuade Jack to re-think his decision about …?
- Is there anything I can do to assist you?

In the coaching situation, the employee is given the opportunity to assess her performance, formulate her own solutions and is empowered to act, with the support of her manager.

Coaching Relationship

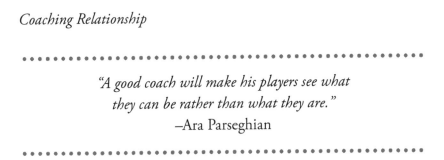

*"A good coach will make his players see what
they can be rather than what they are."*
–Ara Parseghian

Organizations with a coaching culture are more likely to attract star performers who are innovative, use their own initiative, and are more loyal.[14] Through extensive research, Google found that being a good coach was one of the most important skills that predicted effective management.[15] A coaching relationship in which leaders connect with their employees on a personal level is an opportunity to build a stronger, more trusting connection. (Trust is essential in a successful coaching relationship. See Chapter 5 for more information on trust).

Coaching ought to become a leader's habit. It can occur anywhere, at any time – any interaction is a coaching opportunity and gives the manager a chance to give on-the-spot, informal feedback. These coachable moments, by allowing the team member to come up with his own ideas for resolving the issue, results in greater employee empowerment and accountability.

* *

"What sets great leaders apart from good leaders is the ability to identify or create coaching moments on a daily basis."
–GP Strategies

* *

BlessingWhite found that for managers, the biggest obstacles to coaching were (1) that they didn't have enough time, and (2) they didn't have all the answers.[14]

1. The first issue – not having enough time – highlights the fact that some leaders may not realize just how effective coaching can contribute to the bottom line as it enhances productivity and engagement. In the long-term, coaching makes the manager's job easier, so it's imperative to find the time to coach team members.

2. The second obstacle – they don't have all the answers – indicates that managers don't understand the concept of coaching. Coaching doesn't mean you have all the right answers – it's more important that you are asking the right questions! This is the "secret sauce of great coaching." [16] BlessingWhite found that employees appreciated it when managers—rather than being too directive—had a more collaborative approach and helped them generate their own solutions (as illustrated in the scenario above). When employees are coached through the process and develop their own solutions, there is greater buy-in too.

This same (BlessingWhite) research found that leaders who coached reported benefits like enhanced team performance. Of the employees who were coached, 72% claimed that it increased work performance, and 68% stated that satisfaction at work was enhanced. So, it's a win-win-win situation – for team members, for managers, and for the organization.

It's interesting to note that in this study, and a previous one, (the researchers compared their 2016 and 2009 results), BlessingWhite found that the same three coaching behaviors, in the same order, were considered important by both the managers who coached and the employees whom they coached:

1. Clear and candid communication
2. Well-defined performance objectives
3. Keeping promises

See Chapters 1 and 6 for some information on communication. We addressed goal setting earlier in this chapter. The last issue, keeping promises, is part of both the trust issue (covered in Chapter 5), and authenticity (addressed in Chapter 6).

Reflection:

Assess yourself on the critical coaching behaviors:

1. *Is your communication clear and candid? If not, how could you change your communication?*
2. *Do you establish well-defined performance objectives with your employees? If not, how could you ensure you do so going forward?*

> 3. *Do you keep your promises? If not, how could you do so in the future?*

Two other coaching behaviors that were rated higher by employees than their managers included the communication of experiences and personal insights, and keeping employees informed about other opportunities in the organization (including necessary qualifications for promotions, etc.). Do you share your work experiences and learnings with your team members? The second item points to the fact that managers need to be able to let go of the employees that they've developed and encourage and support them as they move upwards or laterally (as mentioned in Chapter 2).

GROW Coaching Model

There are many different coaching models. Obviously, if your organization has already adopted a specific one, you will use that model. However, if your company doesn't have a model, here's one you can use.

The GROW coaching model, popularized by Sir John Whitmore,[17] is a goal setting and performance model that has been used extensively over the last twenty-five years.

		QUESTIONS YOU CAN ASK AT EACH PHASE
G	**GOAL SETTING** • Define the goal • Ensure it is SMART (Specific, Measurable, Attainable, Realistic and Time-bound)	• What is the goal for this discussion? • What goal do you want to achieve? • What is important to you? • How can you make the goal SMART?
R	**REALITY** • Explore the current situation • What is the here and now? Where are we starting from?	• What is the situation now? • What is the gap between where you are and where you want to go? • Have you taken any steps towards your goal? • What has contributed to your success so far? • What is working well at the moment?
O	**OPTIONS** • Brainstorm all ways to achieve the goal – Identify as many options as possible • Generate solutions • Evaluate the pros and cons of each alternative strategy • Select a strategy	• How can you get from here to there? • How have you handled this kind of situation in the past? • What haven't you tried yet? • What else could you do? • Which options do you like? • What are the pros and cons of each option? • Which option will you take?

| W | **WHAT WILL YOU DO? (THE WAY FORWARD)**

• What will the team member commit to next to achieve the goal?
• Create an action plan
• What are the potential obstacles? What will the team member do to overcome them?
• Agree to a follow up / feedback plan | • Does this option meet your objectives?
• What is your first step?
• What subsequent actions do you need to take, and by when?
• Who else can help you?
• What additional resources do you need?
• What potential obstacles do you foresee?
• How will you overcome these obstacles?
• What is your overall plan?
• How can I help with subsequent follow-up or feedback?
• Anything else you want to talk about? |

Remember that throughout the coaching process, you will be asking questions so the employees can become more aware, explore the situation, and discover their own solutions.

When you look at the GROW model, it might seem overwhelming. You can't be expected to remember the various questions for each stage. If you're having a scheduled meeting with your employee, you can plan ahead and – for each of the four components – think of one or two appropriate questions to ask.

However, sometimes coaching happens "on the fly" – a teachable coaching moment occurs. The primary thing to remember is that you shouldn't be giving advice or direction (unless it's an emergency). These coaching moments are an opportunity for you to step back – merely ask questions so the team member generates her own solution/s. Here's what this may look like:

Grow   What do you want to achieve?

Reality   Where are you at right now? (Here, you're helping the employee to determine the gap between the current state and what they want to achieve.)

Options   How could you close the gap/get from here to there? What are the pros and cons of the options you're considering? Which option will you go with?

Way Forward   What is your first step? And the next one? How can I help you? Why don't you create an action plan and think about the possible obstacles and how you will overcome them? If you want, we can get together to review it.

See Tool 4.1 – A list of additional coaching questions you can use.

Are you an effective coach, giving your employees the support they need? Are you ensuring you spend the time necessary to successfully coach your employees? Are you concerned that you don't have all the right answers? Are you able to flex your coaching style to ensure you can get the best out of each of your team members (each of whom have different needs)?

See Tool 4.2 – A checklist to prompt your reflections about your coaching ability.

Accountability

Before reading further, assess your accountability skills by completing the survey below, using the scale:

Never (N), Rarely (R), Sometimes (S), Often (O) and Always (A).

At the bottom of the table, total the number of times you circle each letter. Consider your pattern:

- Which behaviors are you often or always doing? These indicate areas of strength for you.
- Which behaviors are you never or rarely doing? These suggest behaviors that you should try to do more frequently.

Rating	Accountability
N R S O A	1. I focus on results.
N R S O A	2. I hold my team members accountable for meeting expectations and goals.
N R S O A	3. I immediately address any issues of poor performance.
N R S O A	4. I am able to deliver tough and honest feedback.
N R S O A	5. Team members know I expect them to hold each other (and myself) accountable.
N R S O A	6. I expect my team members to try and resolve conflict issues themselves before coming to me.

• •

"We lead in safety because we lead in accountability—not only as it relates to safety but as it relates to everything else we do."
–Mike Wildfong, General Manager, TI Automotive

• •

According to the business dictionary, accountability is "The obligation of an individual or organization to account for its activities, accept responsibility for them, and to disclose the results in a transparent manner." Some authors go even further, saying that it is a personal choice in which people take ownership to achieve the organization's goals/results; they "see it, own it, solve it, and do it." [18] The cornerstone of accountability involves clear expectations/agreements – before problems arise. One report discusses the five talents great managers possess.[2] The ability to create a culture of accountability is one of these talents. Engaging leaders have a performance/results focus, and this ensures that employees are held accountable – these managers promptly address issues of poor performance and manage difficult people and conflict situations.[8] However, one study found that only 40% of the workers surveyed strongly agreed that their managers held them accountable for their performance objectives.[6]

Reflection:

Suppose one of your employees has agreed to a specific goal. He thinks he's doing okay, but you know he's underperforming. How would you handle this situation?

Research demonstrated that accountability is of vital importance to highly engaged employees.[19] In the study, they compared how the drivers of engagement differed between the 10% most engaged employees, the 20% most engaged employees, and all employees. For the 10% of highly engaged employees, the fifth and sixth drivers were around accountability (poor performance being addressed effectively throughout the organization and employees being accountable for meeting expectations and goals). However, when all employees are included in the results, none of the accountability-related issues appear in the top ten. Engaged employees know they are committed to achieving organizational and departmental goals and want everyone to be held accountable for a high level of performance. If this doesn't happen, engaged employees will move to an organization where their goal achievement will be appreciated. If you want to retain your high potentials and star performers, a culture of individual accountability is essential.

Peer Accountability

• •

"In the worst organizations no one holds anyone accountable,
in the good organizations the boss holds people accountable,
*and **in the best organizations everyone holds everyone***
accountable."
–Al Switzler, New York Times bestselling author

• •

We all know how it feels if other team members aren't pulling their weight and so are not achieving project deliverables. We become disengaged and start to feel unenthusiastic about working on the team. We may complain to our teammates about our other colleague, but that doesn't help the situation. On the other hand, when we hold each other accountable, we feel more engaged with the team – we're motivated and feel satisfied and secure.

Reflection:

Think back to the various teams you have worked on. How engaged were you when:

   a. The team members didn't hold each other accountable?
   b. The team members held each other accountable?

Grenny has studied teamwork in organizations and found an interesting relationship between performance and accountability[20] – just like the Al Switzler quote above. In teams with the poorest performance, there is no accountability; in teams with average performance, the supervisor holds team members accountable; in the highest performing teams, team members hold each other accountable. These high performing teams have been empowered to handle poor performance issues with each other politely, openly and as quickly as possible. They call each other out to discuss differences/issues. Peer accountability – a crucial component of team cohesiveness – has been demonstrated to be a strong predictor of various indicators – safety, productivity, quality, efficiency and employee satisfaction.

Case Example – Team Accountability[21]

A consultant was having his first meeting at a very successful financial institution with the CEO and his direct reports. He hadn't met the CEO, but assumed it was the person sitting at the head of the table – especially as this person called out a late-comer ("I thought we'd all agreed that the meeting was starting at 10 a.m., and it's now 10.06 a.m. ..."). A participant explained why her department had fallen short on some sales goals. Another participant asked her some tough questions and gave constructive feedback. The meeting continued in this manner, with different participants asking questions, commenting, and giving respectful feedback.

When the meeting was over, the consultant found out that the CEO was the person who had been the quietest during the whole meeting. He hadn't needed to call anyone out as the team members were holding each other accountable. The team members were firm in their expectations and tough questioning, but they were also understanding and considerate towards each other. They were a high performing team. This CEO had created a culture of "universal accountability."

Some actions you can take to create a culture of accountability:

- Clear expectations – team members know that you expect them to hold each other (and you) accountable.
- Open communication – team members are empowered to address each other when they have issues rather than complain behind their colleague's back.
- Recount positive examples when employees have addressed concerns with each other.
- Model accountability – make sure you hold your employees accountable; and also address concerns you may have with your peers (rather than complaining to your staff about them).
- Have regular check-ins with the team to ensure things are running smoothly.

- Encourage team members to develop new skills and learn from their mistakes.
- If employees complain to you about their teammates, encourage them to address the situation themselves first.
- Have an "it-takes-two-to-escalate" policy.21 Before the issue is brought to you, both parties agree that they aren't able to resolve it between them, and they both want you to step in and help them settle the concern.

Reflection: As a manager –

- *How do you hold your employees accountable?*
- *How do your team members hold each other accountable?*
- *When working with other people (peers) and teams, how do you hold each other accountable?*

Performance Improvement Management:

Now let's look at the performance improvement aspect of accountability. In one study, employees assessed their managers on their ability to help a team member improve poor performance. Even though this skill is very important to employees, they rated their managers as not being very effective when handling these situations.[13] So, it seems that when team members want to improve their performance, their managers are inadequate at providing the necessary coaching to put them on the right track. How would you assess your ability to support your team members when their performance is below expectations?

There are many reasons why an employee's performance falls short (inadequate resources, substandard communication, not using their strengths, conflict, burnout, etc.). Assuming those obstacles have been overcome, the other two major issues in any poor performance situation are (1) Is the employee <u>able</u> to do it? (2) Is the employee <u>willing</u> to do it? In other words, does the employee have the skill/ability to do it, and is the employee motivated to do it? These are two very different questions, which we'll address now in more detail.

1. Is the Employee Able to do it?
   a. The employee may not have the physical ability to do it – maybe he is not strong enough, or dexterous enough, or he is too tall or too short (e.g., there's a minimum height requirement for airline cabin-crew members). In this case, he shouldn't have been given the job in the first place!
   b. Does the employee have the knowledge to do it? If not, how can he be given the knowledge?
   c. Does the employee have the skill/ability? If not, can he be trained to do it?

2. Is the Employee Willing to do it? Has the employee done the work up to standard before? (If so, it means that you answered "yes" to question #1.). Therefore, it must be a willingness/motivation issue. Possible reasons why the employee is no longer motivated to perform:
   a. Boredom with the work (he's been doing it for a long time and/or doesn't find it challenging). Can you re-craft the work so it's more stimulating?
   b. Lack of or loss of passion about the work. Perhaps the employee is also not using his strengths fully. Can you re-craft the work so it's more in line with the employee's strengths/passions?
   c. Lack of accountability. The employee doesn't really see why he needs to work up to standard anymore. What

are the consequences for this? How will you hold the employee accountable?

   d. Personal problems – can you make temporary accommodations?

   e. Conflicts at work – how can these conflicts be resolved so the team member gets back on track?

In any of these situations, you need to have a performance improvement discussion with your team member.

Steps for a Performance Improvement Conversation

1. State the issue – describe the purpose of the conversation with a compassionate, clear and direct approach. Be specific, objective, and timely.
2. Explain the impact on you, the department and the organization.
3. Ask for the team member's perspective, then LISTEN!
4. Ask questions / clarify – so you understand the employee's point of view; be curious. Show you've heard and understood.
5. What is preventing the employee from meeting goals and desired performance levels?
6. How can the employee leverage her strengths?
7. What resources can you and the organization provide to support the process?
8. Seek a shared understanding – what are the desired outcomes you and your employee want?
9. Explore resolutions for all desired outcomes.
10. Discuss options.
11. Establish a performance improvement plan with a timeline.
12. Agree to a plan to review progress at specific intervals.

Afterwards, reflect: *What was effective? What could have been done differently?*

DEEPER DIVE

Let's re-visit the Talent Development Matrix (introduced in Chapter 2):

Talent Development Matrix

POTENTIAL	HIGH POTENTIAL	**7. PARADOX** • Underperformer • Maybe in the wrong role • Maybe bad fit with manager	**8. FUTURE STAR** • Achieves goals • Valued contributor • Potential for growth	**9. SUPER STAR** • Exceeds targets • Future leader • Strong candidate for promotion
		• What's impeding their performance? • Change role/ manager? • Coach – performance manage*; offboard if no improvement	• Challenge – provide leadership and stretch assignments • Provide a mentor • Reward and engage	• Provide special development opportunities • Reward and recognize • Challenge and engage
	EVOLVING POTENTIAL	**4. UNDER-PERFORMER** • Underperformer • Obstacles to performance? • Questionable fit	**5. KEY PLAYER** • Achieves goals • Some potential for growth • Needs greater challenges	**6. CURRENT STAR** • Exceeds targets • Valued contributor • Potential for growth

POTENTIAL	EVOLVING POTENTIAL	• What's impeding their performance? • Challenge them • Coach – performance manage*; offboard if no improvement	• Provide coaching and development opportunities • Provide stretch assignments	• Actively develop for next level • Provide a mentor • Provide development and growth opportunities
	REACHED POTENTIAL	**1. MARGINAL** • Underperformer • Unlikely to improve	**2. SOLID PERFORMER** • Achieves goals • Steady contributor • Content with status quo	**3. FUNCTIONAL EXPERT** • Exceeds targets • Loves job • Content with status quo
		• Performance manage*; offboard if no improvement	• Motivate and engage • Discuss their future goals • Provide resources for consistent performance	• Engage, challenge and reward • Discuss their future goals • Can mentor others, share their knowledge
		LOW Unacceptable	AVERAGE Meets expectations	HIGH Exceeds expectations
		PERFORMANCE		

In this section, we're focusing on the employees who are performing below expectations – those in boxes 1, 4 and 7. The manager needs to hold the employees accountable for their sub-par performance, which should be addressed right away. The leader ought to have a coaching discussion around the performance gap and collaboratively develop an action plan / a performance improvement plan.

Employees in Box 1 are the Marginal performers who have already reached their potential and have performance problems. Have a performance improvement conversation with them and follow up on their action plan/performance improvement plan. This gives them the opportunity to move from low to acceptable performance. If there is no improvement, consider termination.

Employees in Box 4 are Under-Performers. They have some potential but are performing at an unacceptable level. Is it an ability or motivational issue? Perhaps it's a questionable fit with the work/department/manager/culture. Are there other performance obstacles? Do they need more challenging work? Are they not fully using their strengths? Have a performance improvement conversation with them. How could you both work together so their performance improves? Follow up on their action plan/performance improvement plan. If there is no improvement, consider reassignment or termination.

Employees in Box 7 – Paradox – are high potentials, but why aren't they working up to standard? As mentioned above, perhaps it's a questionable fit with the work/department/manager/culture. These employees could be future Super Stars. Can you change their role, or parts of it so it's a better fit, they are more fully using their strengths, or they can work on projects they are more passionate about? Will more challenging work turn the situation around? Should they be accommodated in a different department? Are there other performance obstacles? Have a performance improvement conversation with them and follow up on their action plan/performance improvement plan. The organization doesn't want to lose a future super star. However, if there is no improvement, consider reassignment or termination.

The important issue is that you first have a coaching discussion with individual employees to motivate them to improve their performance. Monitor their progress and give them feedback. However, you have to hold your employees accountable for their performance. At the end of the day – if there is no improvement, they may need to be terminated. Do make sure, though, that you've first tried to uncover any possible obstacles to acceptable performance and considered a change in work tasks/role. If this is a situation of firing the employee, you need to follow your organization's policy regarding terminations.

Reflection:

- *How do you handle work performance that is below par?*
- *What do you usually do to help employees improve their performance?*
- *If a specific employee's performance doesn't improve, should he still be working for you? How will you handle that situation?*

Formal Review Discussion:

In this book, we won't address the steps in holding a formal review discussion, but just note some important issues regarding the annual review and employee performance.

The Corporate Leadership Council did some extensive research (as mentioned before).[21] They examined 106 performance management strategies, and categorized these strategies into "A," "B," "C," and "D" – level drivers. The nine A-level drivers had the capacity to increase performance by 25% or more. The third highest driver was "Emphasis (in formal review) on performance strengths," and this potentially increased performance by **36.4%**. Therefore, it will serve you well to ensure you have a strengths focus during the review discussion. On the other hand, the D-level strategies negatively impacted performance. See the figure below which shows the maximum impact on performance for the D-level drivers related to feedback/performance reviews.

Rank Order	Performance Driver	Impact on Performance
102	Emphasis (in informal feedback) on personality weaknesses	(3.2%)
103	Emphasis (in formal review) on personality weaknesses	(5.5%)
104	Emphasis (in informal feedback) on performance weaknesses	(10.9%)
105	Emphasis (in formal review) on performance weaknesses	(26.8%)

Figure 4.1: Impact of Manager's Action on Employee's Performance

As you can see from this table, most of these strategies centered on the emphasis of performance or personality weaknesses. At #105 – with the potential of a negative 26.8% – is the emphasis – in a formal review – on performance weaknesses. This highlights the necessity – both during formal reviews and informal feedback – of NOT focusing on personality or performance weaknesses. It is okay to mention them, but the performance review discussion should rather be concentrating on the future and how you will help to develop your employee. (You should have already addressed poor performance at the time it occurred.)

The good news is that the four items in the table above are within your control. Rather than a negative impact on productivity, you can have a positive impact (up to 36.4%) on your team members' performance by emphasizing their performance strengths during formal reviews. (See Chapter 3 for information on leading from a strengths perspective.)

Should Performance Management Systems be Scrapped?

Let's end this chapter with this important question! Obviously, you may not have the authority to scrap the performance management system, but it's useful to know the reasons some organizations are doing so or thinking about doing so.

There are two major problems with the annual performance review: firstly, its focus is retrospective – appraising what has already occurred – and some events occurred ten, eleven or twelve months ago. Secondly (and it's related to the first), employees aren't getting real-time feedback. Both of these issues can be alleviated if feedback is given in a timely manner – as close to the performance event as possible. Also, technology (such as feedback apps, crowd-sourced feedback, pulse tools, etc.) can be leveraged so employees are more participative in the process and can monitor their own progress through frequent online updates.

Performance management was found to be effective by 45% of employers and only a third of managers and employees were satisfied with the process.[22] Other research found that only 14% of workers strongly agreed that their reviews motivated them to perform more effectively.[23] Despite these results, only about a quarter of the companies surveyed are thinking of discarding performance ratings, and just 11% are determining whether to scrap the performance management system entirely. However, some companies are discarding the annual review and ranking system in favor of continuous coaching discussions about performance, with a focus on potential contribution.[24] This emphasis on coaching illustrates the movement from retrospective feedback to forward-focusing coaching.

According to Finkelstein,[25] GE have revamped their performance management system. Now during appraisals, employees are given feedback so they know what they should "continue" to do, and also behaviors they should "consider" doing in a different way. Again, this demonstrates the more future-oriented aspects of coaching, and that managers are more collaborative and not as directive as they were previously – asking employees to "consider" different behaviors rather than telling them "don't do this!"

Case Example – Adobe – Eliminating Annual Performance Reviews[26]

Adobe calculated that it was dedicating 80,000 manager hours to its annual performance review process. The company didn't feel there were getting much in return. In fact, every February, after the reviews were completed, there was an increase in the number of employee resignations (because employees felt jaded and undervalued and were disappointed in their appraisals).

An Adobe executive – Donna Morris – decided to eliminate the cumbersome annual performance review process altogether. It took the company a while to figure out a replacement. Now they have a "Check-in" system – managers and employees have multiple Check-in conversations each year, addressing quarterly goals, feedback and career development. Best of all, there isn't any tracking or documentation! There is also an annual Rewards Check-in, from which managers recommend salary increases based on performance.

Since the implementation of the Check-in system, employee engagement and empowerment has increased and turnover has dramatically decreased.

Takeaways

- Organizations achieve their goals through effective performance management.
- Collaborative goal setting is at the core of performance management.
- Ensure your team members understand how their work aligns with the organization's goals.
- Feedback/coaching should be ongoing.
- Ensure your feedback/coaching is future-focused and developmental.
- Ask questions so your employees can discover their own solutions.
- Focus on results.
- Foster a culture of universal accountability – hold everyone (including yourself and your peers) accountable.
- In annual reviews, focus on employee strengths and developmental opportunities.

Tool 4.1 – Coaching Questions

Here are the coaching questions mentioned in the scenario earlier in the chapter:

- How did you feel when …?
- Are you satisfied with your response?
- What might you have done differently?
- What can you do to prepare for that kind of issue in the future?
- Is there anything you could do now to persuade Jack to re-think his decision about …?
- Is there anything I can do to assist you?

Here are some additional questions:

- Can you tell me more?
- What factors led you to …?
- What do you need so you can take that step?
- What outcome would make this successful?
- When have you reacted like this in the past?
- What steps have you taken in the past in similar situations?
- How could you use your strengths to handle this?
- How would you like to proceed?
- What course of action would you like to take?
- What other actions could you take?
- Anything else you can think of?
- Are there any obstacles in the way of your success?
- Are there other people you could involve in this?

- Which would you rather do?
- Do you need any additional resources?
- How important is this to you?
- Do you think that's realistic?
- What makes this difficult?
- What impact do you think it had on the other person?

Tool 4.2 – Coaching Ability Checklist

Here is a checklist to prompt your reflections about your coaching ability:

- [ ] Do your employees trust you?
- [ ] Do you have a close connection with each of your team members?
- [ ] Are you an engaged listener?
- [ ] Do you spend enough time coaching your team members?
- [ ] Do you seek opportunities where you can assist your employees to work more effectively?
- [ ] Do you set clear development/coaching goals?
- [ ] Are the goals focused on business outcomes?
- [ ] Do you help your employees see the connection between their work and the organization's mission and strategic goals?
- [ ] Are you collaborative rather than directive?
- [ ] Do you tailor your coaching to each direct report?
- [ ] Are you holding people accountable – measuring and tracking results?
- [ ] Do you know how to coach your star performers to even higher levels of performance?
- [ ] Do you know how to coach your team members whose performance is below standard?
- [ ] Rather than specifying your own solutions, do you ask questions, giving your employees the time to reflect and figure out how they could do things differently in the future?
- [ ] Do you share your personal insights?

- [ ] Do you share your experiences?
- [ ] How can you use coaching opportunities to boost productivity?
- [ ] Do you provide frequent coaching to your team members?
- [ ] Do you apprise your employees about promotional opportunities in the organization and help them understand specific skill requirements?
- [ ] Do your employees feel that your coaching is valuable?
- [ ] Do you follow through on any commitments you've made?
- [ ] Are you using recognition to reinforce effective performance?

- [ ] Are you coached by your manager?
- [ ] Have you been trained on how to coach?
- [ ] Do the executives in your organization coach?

Chapter 5

Be Inclusive

*"The demand for deliberately inclusive workplace practices,
behaviors and environments will grow as employees continue
to elevate their needs and expectations. Leaders will be held
accountable to address these demands."*
–Liz McAuliffe, EVP Human Resources, T-Mobile

*"We need to resist the tyranny of low expectations. We need to
open our eyes to the inequality that remains."*
–Sheryl Sandberg, COO, Facebook

Humans are social beings. We crave being with others and belonging to one or more social groups. A large part of our identity is tied up with personal and professional groups, particularly our work groups and organizations as a whole. As today's environment becomes more diverse and global, the experience of being included or excluded at work will have an impact on our engagement and performance.

In this chapter, we will talk about the meaning of inclusion, how it is related to engagement and what leaders and managers can do to be more inclusive, so as to better engage their employees and enhance workplace productivity. We underscore the importance of fostering psychological safety, and we discuss four inclusive leader behaviors, namely being open, curious and adaptable; acting fairly; behaving authentically; and relating with empathy.

First, let's define some terms, specifically inclusion, and an often-related concept, diversity. Even though these two concepts are linked, they are not the same thing. Diversity refers to the range and mix of employees represented in the organization, in terms of their ideas, backgrounds and cultural dimensions. Diversity dimensions include both visible and invisible categories such as gender, race, nationality, sexual orientation, religion, educational background, family status, and so on. Inclusion refers to the degree to which employees feel they are fully integrated into their organizations and can participate in all important aspects of organizational functioning.[1]

Underlying inclusion are trust, fairness and respect. At work, inclusion means being able to connect successfully with colleagues, having access to vital information and having a say in decision-making that matters. It also means being treated and rewarded equitably. Fully inclusive work cultures are high-performing environments that leverage the talents of their diverse employees to maximize business outcomes.

Nowadays, organizations may call themselves diverse in terms of the membership of employees from various cultural categories. However, can all organizations claim that their diverse members truly feel "included"? Feeling included is a different story from feeling represented. One diversity consultant notes the difference between diversity and inclusion is that "Diversity is being invited to the party; Inclusion is being asked to dance." [2]

For instance, imagine the experience of a sole female executive who is not invited by her male colleagues to the golf course and is excluded from a night out at the club. Imagine her dismay upon coming to work the next day to hear her male colleagues trading inside jokes and casually mentioning that they've already made a number of decisions while playing golf and drinking in the club. A more contemporary example is depicted in the movie "The Intern." Robert de Niro plays a retired executive from a very traditional industry who decides to apply for an internship at an online fashion start-up headed by a young female played by Anne Hathaway. The employees are all Millennials. Talk about feeling lost at the speed and informality of the start-up culture and feeling out of place for not having a Twitter or Facebook account! Fortunately, the younger employees, particularly Anne Hathaway, were eventually able to appreciate, utilize and benefit from Robert de Niro's deep experience and talents, though not before many awkward and comedic moments.

Diversity and inclusion thus mean not just being nice to people from different groups or doing the moral thing. Fortune 500 companies, compared to other companies, were more likely to invest in diversity and inclusion for strategic business reasons, such as increasing employee engagement, enhancing organizational innovation and agility, and maximizing talent acquisition. Yet while many senior leaders agree diversity and inclusion are important, only 11% of companies classify themselves as truly inclusive. And only 23% of companies hold their CEO's accountable for achieving diversity and inclusion (D&I) objectives.[3] Moreover, according to a recent global and diversity survey, diversity (or specifically, the failure to manage diversity) is seen as a barrier to employee progression in their organizations; this perception is particularly true among younger workers (age 18-29 years) compared to workers above 60.[4]

Reflection:

It would be helpful for us to reflect on the following questions in order to better appreciate the link between inclusion and engagement in our own work environments:[5]

- *Think of a time when you were with a group at work wherein you felt included and heard. You felt you really belonged. Why do you think you felt included? How did this affect your energy and focus? How engaged were you? How would you rate your performance and contributions to the group?*
- *Now think of a time when you felt like an outsider at work. You felt different. You felt isolated, hardly acknowledged, heard or understood. Why do you think you felt excluded? How did this affect your energy and focus? How engaged were you? How would you rate your performance and contributions to the group?*
- *Can you think of specific examples where you have noticed employees at work being included or excluded? How did this affect their engagement and performance?*

Leadership at all levels plays a crucial role in creating and sustaining inclusive cultures within their organizations. This happens at both the strategic level as well as on a day-to-day level.

Take a moment to assess the extent to which you are an inclusive leader in your workplace by completing the survey below, using the scale:

Never (N), Rarely (R), Sometimes (S), Often (O) and Always (A).

At the bottom of the table, total the number of times you circle each letter. Consider your pattern:

- Which behaviors are you often or always doing? These indicate areas of strength for you.
- Which behaviors are you never or rarely doing? These suggest behaviors that you should try to do more frequently.

Rating	Inclusive Leadership
N R S O A	1. I am curious to learn about the interests and experiences of my team members.
N R S O A	2. I intentionally seek diverse perspectives.
N R S O A	3. I create a safe environment where team members can express themselves fully.
N R S O A	4. I build a team where team members feel a strong sense of belongingness.
N R S O A	5. I treat each team member with respect and fairness.
N R S O A	6. I ensure that my team members feel valued.
N R S O A	7. I am aware of my values and potential biases.
N R S O A	8. I build relationships across individuals and groups.

N R S O A	9. I create common goals to unite individuals and groups.

The Link between Inclusion and Employee Engagement

Empirical research on the relationship between inclusion and engagement is actually quite new, with few published studies as of yet. Interestingly, when Gallup first published its Q12 Engagement Survey, the most controversial item in that survey was "I have a best friend at work." Academicians, consultants and managers had previously scoffed at the relevance of this item. But in the last few years, with increasing attention on the concept of inclusion plus some emerging findings on the significant correlation between inclusion and engagement, it could very well turn out that Gallup will have the last laugh on this item. For example, there is, in fact, research indicating the significant relationship between workplace friendships and employee engagement[6] as well the links among inclusion, trust, and employee engagement.[7]

Indeed, there is a strong conceptual basis for the relationship between inclusion and engagement. Most of us are familiar with Maslow's hierarchy of needs, which states that human beings have five levels of human needs that drive motivation[8]. These needs must be satisfied in a sequential level, starting with physiological needs, safety and security, love and belongingness, self-esteem, and self-actualization. Inclusion is represented in Maslow's hierarchy by the need for love and belongingness. This is true even today. A recent Wall Street Journal article called attention to the fact that today's employees value the sense of belongingness more than material perks at work.[9]

A more contemporary model, self-determination theory, highlights relatedness (the opportunity to build close meaningful relationships with others) as one of three fundamental human needs that fuel psychological well-being and peak functioning.[10] This theory underscores that connecting with others and being cared for by people can be just as important for our mental health and performance as the ability to make choices (autonomy) and demonstrate our mastery (competence).

Finally, Kahn's theory of work engagement lists three psychological drivers of engagement: psychological safety, meaningfulness and availability (in terms of one's energy and resources).[11] Inclusion is related to all three but most obviously to *psychological safety*. When employees feel included in the work group or organization, they feel trusted and valued. They feel safe to express themselves fully and are not cognitively or emotionally hampered by concerns about supervisory or peer doubts, insecurities, interpersonal competition, prejudice and/or envy. There is a sense that it is okay to be imperfect and vulnerable because the people around are supportive and nurturing.

Ferdman writes about inclusion as the capacity to bring one's "whole self" to work.[12] This is an important notion with powerful implications about engagement. When employees feel fully valued, they have more *availability* (i.e., more energy, focus and creativity) for themselves and others. Employees are free to be themselves. Because they trust in the acceptance of others, they can spend more time connecting and sharing their diverse talents with others instead of feeling vulnerable and uncertain. This results in the creation of a strong web of positive interpersonal ties within and across the organization, which allows more open sharing of important social, intellectual and material resources among employees. This increases the physical, mental and psychological availability and confidence of employees to achieve specific challenging goals, thereby enhancing their engagement and productivity.

Employees who feel included are closely connected to others and their organization as a whole. They have a deeper sense of appreciation of the purpose of their work and how their individual jobs feed into the group's and organization's mission and vision (meaningfulness). They identify strongly with their organization (their "in-group" as social psychologists would say). Included employees are more likely to subscribe to the values of their organization, and are proud supporters, even promoters of their companies. A popular term in talent management is employee branding. Companies that have a strong employee brand have a very positive and visible presence in the marketplace, not just among their customers but also among employees who are fanatical about their organizations, are extremely loyal, and actively and voluntarily promote their organizations to others- all of which indicate strong employee engagement.

Research by the Institute for Employment Studies has shown that the strongest predictor of engagement was the sense of feeling involved and valued.[13] This includes: employee involvement in decision making; the ability to voice ideas with managers who listen and value such contributions; the growth opportunities employees have to develop in their jobs; and the extent to which the organization demonstrates concern for employee health and well-being. Within safe, supportive and inclusive environments, there is no tolerance for favoritism and cliques; employees believe their talents and contributions will be fairly recognized and rewarded, further fueling positive feelings about their work and the organization. Organizations that are more inclusive tend to have employees who not only think highly of their organizations, but they go out of their way to be helpful to colleagues and generally act as good citizens of their organizations.[14]

Being included may be even more critical in today's high-tech society. Despite of (or maybe *because* of) the advances of technology and social media, it can be very easy to "connect" with others. However, many of these connections are not necessarily deep and meaningful. It is one thing to have thousands of followers, but how many really know you at a meaningful level? How many really care?

PwC (a global consulting firm) commissioned a NextGen study to understand what motivates and empowers Millennials.[15] Their study found that Millennials are driven more by flexible work environments and a sense of community, appreciation and team collaboration, compared to Gen Xer's, who valued control over work, opportunities for development and rewards/compensation more. Meanwhile, there is an interesting phenomenon called "ghosting" in the workplace, wherein employees (notoriously many Millennials) literally stop coming to work and are impossible to reach. We suspect (as do other workplace experts) that employees might be having issues, feel unheard, excluded or undervalued and are uncomfortable speaking with their bosses. While such behavior looks unprofessional, it appears that these employees would rather leave than engage in meaningful conversation with their leaders. Moreover, with a tight labor market, there are other job opportunities for them.[16]. Unfortunately, it is the organizations that lose out on their investment in hiring and training such employees. The phenomenon of ghosting suggests that leaders and organizations that can do a better job of building a strong sense of community through inclusive efforts can increase employee engagement, retention and ultimately, performance.

Business Outcomes of Inclusion and Engagement

Does investing in inclusion really contribute to concrete business outcomes? Downy, Werff, Thomas and Plaut investigated the role of diversity practices and inclusion in promoting trust and employee engagement in a large healthcare organization.[7] Their results showed that the more employees think their leaders and organizations support diversity-related efforts (e.g., recruiting diverse job candidates, implementing strong anti-harassment and discrimination procedures), the more they consider their work climate to be high in trust, which leads to a higher level of engagement. This is particularly true for employees who feel included.

Inclusive leaders have a big impact on individual employee engagement and productivity. An eighteen-month study of employees from companies such as Citicorp, Fujitsu and the British Army, revealed that over 80% of employees working for inclusive leaders have higher levels of motivation, loyalty and productivity.[17] Another study reported a positive link between inclusive leadership and the likelihood that employees engage in helping behaviors toward their leaders and workgroups, especially when the diversity climate of the organization was positive. Not surprisingly, this finding is stronger among ethnic minorities and women.[18] Still another study across six countries indicated that the more included employees feel, the more they report being more innovative in their work as well as being more helpful toward their teams.[19]

At the group level, a highly publicized study at Google stressed the importance of psychological safety and inclusion on team performance and engagement. This initiative, called Project Aristotle, sought to understand what comprises the "perfect" team.[20] After observing, interviewing, and analyzing hundreds of teams, Google's multidisciplinary research team concluded that high-performing teams were not necessarily comprised of the most intelligent or experienced members, nor were they made up of members representing particular sets of personality traits. Rather, Google's high-performing teams operated with certain norms. These unwritten rules or guidelines centered around psychological safety, specifically conversational turn-taking and empathy. Team members believed that everybody's opinions were valuable; it was important for each member to be able to express his or her thoughts, ideas, concerns and objections. Interestingly, members felt secure sharing not only professional information but also personal information, such as serious illness or family situations. In fact, such stories brought team members together and allowed them to get to know each other more fully.

At the organizational level, aligning diversity and inclusion efforts with strategic objectives has important financial consequences. Bersin by Deloitte conducted a survey of 454 organizations (with a combined total revenue of over $750 million) and found that companies with targeted, integrated and inclusive talent activities generated significantly greater cash flow per employee over a three-year period compared to those with less inclusive talent initiatives. Higher-performing companies viewed diverse talent as assets (rather than costs). They invested in creating a culture of learning and implemented leadership-development initiatives at all levels, including critical talent segments. They took into serious consideration diversity and inclusion in all talent initiatives, including recruitment, development, performance management and succession planning.[21]

Additional research by Deloitte has shown that companies with inclusive cultures are six times more likely to be agile and innovative and eight times more likely to hit better business outcomes.[22]

Finally, another top consulting firm analyzed data from more than 1,000 large companies across twelve countries to investigate the link between diverse organizational leadership and financial performance. They found that companies with the highest ethnic diversity among their top executives were 33% more likely to have above-average profitability compared to companies with the least ethnically diverse executive teams. Similarly, companies with the highest level of gender diversity among their top executives were 21% more likely to have above-average profitability compared to those with the least level of executive gender diversity. Those with the lowest levels of both ethnic and gender executive diversity were 29% less likely to hit above-average profitability measures compared to all other companies in the McKinsey study.[23]

The McKinsey report also noted that the companies that stand out in terms of their diversity and inclusion (D&I) efforts were better able to attract the best talent, score higher in employee satisfaction, and have stronger levels of customer service. Executives from these leading companies had a compelling vision for D&I, and these visions were linked with their business growth priorities. Executives also cascaded their vision to managers and built a strong system for accountability to ensure that these D&I initiatives are implemented.[22]

Sodexho, Accenture, and U.S. Bank are three organizations that have been recognized for their diversity and inclusion efforts. They employ various strategies that have yielded positive results in terms of employee retention, engagement, and individual and organizational performance.

Case Examples: Sodexho, Accenture and U.S. Bank

Sodexho is a global organization that provides quality-of-life services ranging from construction, cleaning, reception and food services in various sectors such as hospitals, schools, government offices and business organizations. The company has been recognized for its D&I efforts over the past ten years and was recently inducted into the Hall of Fame by Diversity Inc. Among Sodexho's practices to enhance engagement are organizing employee business resource groups to encourage networking among employees around a shared set of interests and experiences; mentoring programs; training; flexible work arrangements; and the recognition of managers and employees for supporting D&I within the organization.[24]

Sodexho seeks to enhance gender balance at all levels of the company. This objective is a strategic one as a Sodexho internal study had found that business units with greater proportions of women had 10% higher operating margins, client retention and employee retention, and 14% higher employee engagement. Sodexho has put together an advisory board called SoTogether (formerly called SWIFt). This board, which is composed of females and males from seventeen different nationalities, has the objective of achieving 40% female representation in leadership positions by 2025. (The company is currently at 32%.) To reinforce the importance of this objective, Sodexo has linked a proportion of senior leaders' annual bonuses to progress made toward this goal.[25]

Accenture, one of the world's major, professional services/consulting companies, was recently named the top company on the 2018 Thomson Reuters Diversity and Inclusion Index, which lists the 100 most diverse and inclusive companies in the world.[26] This index is based on how companies are rated on diversity, inclusion, people development and news controversy.

Accenture has close to 459,000 employees who serve clients in more than 120 countries. Some of the major actions that Accenture has taken to become a more diverse and inclusive workplace are: a) the creation of a diverse board of directors (with strong gender and global representation); b) female representation (currently women represent 41% of Accenture's workforce, and the company targets a 50% global representation of women by 2025); c) significant investment in talent development (the company spent $935 million in learning and development, including training in key areas such as cloud and artificial intelligence); d) demographic data transparency. Accenture was the first professional services company to voluntarily share its full workforce demographics in the U.S.[27]

Julie Sweet, CEO of Accenture North America, has the task of bringing female representation in the company up to 50%. According to her, diversity is not just about the numbers, but more about inclusion – focusing on what it feels like for employees to come to work everyday. It is about leaders having courageous conversations on topics that matter, such as race. Sweet states that to influence change, companies need to make diversity and inclusion a business priority, and like any priority, they should set goals, prepare action plans, measure progress, and hold leaders accountable. Accenture's mission is "to improve the communities where we work and live." To accomplish this, Sweet says that Accenture leaders must be able to apply their company's core values (e.g., respect and meritocracy) along with their expertise when working with clients and communities.[28]

U.S. Bank is the fifth largest bank in the U.S. and was recently named by Forbes to be a "Best Employer for Diversity" in 2019. This recognition is based on data from employee surveys, reputation assessments, and public diversity leader information. Among the bank's key D&I initiatives are its active hiring of veterans and its supplier diversity program (U.S. Bank has increased its spending on small firms owned by women, minorities, veterans and LGBT suppliers).

In 2016, after the shooting of black motorist Philando Castile in St. Paul, MN, Greg Cunningham (Global VP for Diversity & Inclusion) urged the bank's CEO and its senior leaders to take bold and inclusive action. As a result, U.S. Bank's most senior leaders embarked on cross-country conversation tours to really listen to bank employees at the ground level and to create safe spaces for them to voice ideas and concerns. U.S. Bank also encourages and recognizes senior leaders who serve as outside board members for diverse organizations.[29]

Inclusive Leadership

On a day-to-day basis, what does it mean to be an inclusive leader? We have reviewed various theoretical and empirical articles on inclusive leadership. Indeed, in recent years, a number of models have outlined the qualities or traits of inclusive leaders.[30] We have incorporated ideas from these various sources and we present these in the form of behaviors (rather than innate characteristics that may or may not be learned).

We believe that inclusive leaders demonstrate at least four important behaviors:

- Being open, curious and adaptable
- Acting fairly
- Behaving authentically
- Relating with empathy

These behaviors allow them to create high-trust and high-performance work environments that encourage, draw out and fully maximize diverse talent.

Being Open, Curious and Adaptable

Inclusive leaders are open, genuinely curious and love to learn. They frequently interact with and learn from diverse people. They actively invite others to participate in discussions and decisions; they seek out multiple perspectives, encourage creative ideas, and convey appreciation for people's diverse contributions. For inclusive leaders, diversity is exciting- a potential source of strength, not a threat. These leaders foster inclusion through open communication and flexibility, thus creating safe environments that encourage their followers to exhibit their whole selves at work.[31] The wealth of ideas and perspectives that derive from an inclusive environment leads to greater organizational creativity and performance.

Because inclusive leaders are open and curious, they are able to provide a positive platform for their people to use their strengths. As discussed in Ch. 3, strengths are unique naturally occurring patterns of behaving, thinking, or feeling that are both authentic and energizing to each individual.[32] People are most likely to exhibit the full force of their strengths in situations when they are in a safe haven- when they feel trusted, included, encouraged and appreciated.

We encourage you to test this proposition. Building on the reflection questions at the beginning of this chapter:

- *What strengths were you able to exhibit during the times when you felt included?*
- *Were you able to unleash them to the same extent during the times when you felt excluded?*

For greater impact, make a collective list of the strengths that would be fully unleashed by everyone when your group is a fully inclusive team. This is likely to be a long and impressive list. *See what you stand to gain by investing in inclusion?*

Inclusive leaders are very adaptable. This is because they take an active interest in learning about people from different backgrounds and cultures. They venture out of their comfort zones and volunteer for new experiences in different environments, whether personally or professionally. As such, they develop a broader lens from which to view the world. Through their interest and exposure in different environments, they begin to shed false assumptions and stereotypes, and learn how to view the world from different perspectives. As such, they are more culturally adept in flexing the way they communicate and behave in diverse situations, thus increasing their ability to make individuals and groups feel more included.[33]

Refer to Tool 5.1 and 5.2 for some resources that encourage people to expand their openness, awareness and appreciation about diversity. Tool 5.1 is a Ted Talk by Chimamanda Adichie about the "Danger of a Single Story"; Tool 5.2 is an activity on discovering multiple intelligences.

Acting Fairly

Inclusive leaders are fair-minded. They believe everyone should be treated equally, and should thus have an equal voice. Inclusive leaders are courageous; they do not hesitate to call out and combat blatant or subtle acts of prejudice and discrimination. Unfortunately, in many companies today, not many leaders challenge biased language and discriminatory behaviors when they see them. LeanIn.org and McKinsey did a survey of 279 companies across North America and found that less than 1/3 of employees see their managers speaking out against biased language and behaviors.[34] However, it is when inclusive leaders "go to bat" for their people that employees see how much their leaders care for them. This increases their level of motivation, engagement and organizational commitment.

A number of companies such as PwC, Starbucks and Google are now offering unconscious bias training for managers to enable them to understand how their assumptions may affect the fairness of their decisions and behaviors. Such training typically includes building awareness of stereotyping, prejudice and discrimination, discussing methods to reduce discrimination in hiring, appraising, and promoting employees, and identifying constructive ways to support diversity and inclusion in the workplace.

It is important to note that training is unlikely to work, especially if offered as a one-shot deal. Leaders should be discussing and implementing ways to reduce bias and increase fairness within their teams continuously. For example, Johnson & Johnson integrates discussions of diversity and inclusion at all levels of training, goal setting, performance reviews, and coaching conversations.[35]

Organizations should develop standards and systems to reinforce fair and inclusive decisions and behaviors. For instance, Mozilla developed a code of conduct, Community Participation Guidelines, to promote a positive and safe community for their employees.[36] These guidelines spell out specific behaviors around being respectful, direct but professional, inclusive, accommodating and appreciating similarities and differences, and leading by example. The guidelines also identify specific behaviors that will not be tolerated, including violence or threats of violence, personal attacks and unwanted sexual advances or physical contact.

Inclusive leaders do not play favorites. They look for ways to offer opportunities to everyone on their teams. They coach, mentor and sponsor employees especially from less historically advantaged groups. They have a firm belief in the capabilities of their people regardless of their backgrounds. As an example, co-founder and Executive Chairman of Oracle, Larry Ellison, once helped a receptionist named Anneke Seley learn computer programming. She eventually advanced to senior management and designed Oracle Direct, the company's successful, revolutionary inside-sales department.[37] Moreover, inclusive leaders are able to share authority with others. They are comfortable enabling their employees to take on major responsibilities. At the same time, they are results-oriented and hold people accountable for work commitment.

Reflection:

Have you ever been treated as a second-class citizen at work? How did that make you feel?

When you witnessed disparate treatment of others in the workplace, how did you react? Did you call others out on it?

As a leader, to what extent are you aware of the unique challenges faced by your employees, especially those from minority or historically disadvantaged groups? How can you go about learning more about these employees and meeting their needs?

Behaving Authentically

Inclusive leaders are authentic. They are deeply aware of their own values, biases and assumptions, and strive to ensure that these do not negatively impact others. They are open about how they make decisions, and model integrity in their words and actions. They are not afraid to admit that, sometimes, they don't know everything. They are not afraid to acknowledge mistakes and learn from others. Inclusive and authentic leaders create safe and supportive environments that allow honest, constructive dialogue. (More about authenticity is discussed in Chapter 6.)

Authentic and inclusive leaders use statements and questions like:

- Tell me more about your experience.
- Ask me anything. I'll share what I know.
- I'm not quite sure which direction to take. What would you do if you were in my shoes?
- Here is where I am coming from…I'd like to know your perspective too.
- Here's what's really going on and how it affects you.
- What should we keep doing? What should we stop doing?
- How can we do things differently? (or, What's a better approach?)
- How can I help you?
- What would you like to see?
- It was my call, and I realize it was a mistake…
- I trust you.
- I value your contributions.
- Thank you.

Can you think of other ways for you as a leader to convey authenticity and inclusiveness?

Case Example – Tim Ryan, PwC: The Inclusive CEO[38]

Perhaps one of the most compelling stories of an inclusive leader is that of Tim Ryan, Senior Partner and Chairman of PwC U.S., one of the world's top four accounting firms. Ryan is a fifty-plus white male, one who would typically not be expected to be a standard bearer for race relations in organizations.

Ryan had assumed that his black PwC colleagues (as well as other non-white, non-male colleagues) felt as included and welcomed in PwC as he did. However, in the summer of 2016 when he first took office as head of PwC U.S., there had just been a series of police shootings of black males (i.e., Dallas, Minnesota and Baton Rouge, Louisiana). Ryan sent out an email to check in with his thousands of PwC colleagues around the country and was surprised at the kind of responses he received (i.e., silence from many, but also expressions of isolation and pain from minority employees). He realized how arrogant he had been to assume that his colleagues and employees had the same privileges and experiences as he did.

Ryan decided to initiate formal and informal conversations about race within PwC, and by so doing, he learned how big a gap there was in terms of diversity and inclusion within corporations. He continued to have conversations with minority colleagues no matter how uncomfortable these were, to increase his knowledge, check his assumptions, and learn more from their experiences. In one instance, Ryan shared how he had realized one of his own blind spots. He had been about to fill a senior role in the organization and had initially not planned to mention this opportunity to a female who was a single mother. The role required the person to relocate. Ryan had shared this thought with another male colleague who challenged him not to make this decision for the woman but to allow her to make this decision for herself. This was an "aha" moment for Ryan, who reports humbly, yet proudly, that the woman is doing great work in her new, more senior role.

Ryan felt that CEO's play a critical role in pushing the needle on diversity and inclusion in corporations, and in 2017, he helped found an initiative called CEO Action for Diversity and Inclusion.[39] Today there are more than 550 companies that are part of this coalition whose mission is to rally businesses to take action to build "productive, diverse and inclusive workplaces." One of the coalition's activities was to promote a "Day of Understanding" (December 7, 2018) in which member companies across the U.S. engaged in activities to develop "trusting places for having complex, and sometimes difficult, conversations about diversity and inclusion."

The initiative also has a great website for people and organizations to openly share ideas, actions and experiences to improve diversity and inclusion results. Companies can post information about their practices, from affinity groups to developing diverse talent, mentoring and sponsorship, leadership, metrics and accountability, succession planning, and work/life flexibility and benefits. For instance, related to building leader and employee empathy and authenticity, PwC shares information about its "Blind Spots" training program and Bank of America describes its toolkit for "Courageous Conversations."

Reflection:

When making important decisions, do you seek out diverse perspectives, and make your people aware that you've taken into account these considerations?

Think of a time when your employees raised difficult questions. Were you tense? Defensive? Were you open enough to question your assumptions and make space for an open and constructive dialogue?

When an employee makes a mistake, how do you respond?

As a leader, when you made mistakes, how did you communicate about these mistakes with your people? How did you hope they would respond?

Relating with Empathy

Inclusive leaders are excellent relationship builders. They not only value diversity, but they also know how to foster inclusion through strong, interpersonal and team-building skills. They are great listeners, communicators, and network-builders. They are generous with their connections and introduce people to others. They pay attention to the unique strengths, needs and desires of each team member while building a meaningful shared identity and vision for the team.[40] They know the value of being acknowledged and frequently show their appreciation of others.

What steps can inclusive leaders take to strengthen relationships, especially between highly diverse individuals and groups? One is to engage in meaningful conversations, like Tim Ryan of PwC did as described above. Another obvious solution is to increase the opportunities for diverse individuals and groups to work together so that they begin to empathize and understand each other better. However, it's not as simple as that. Extensive social-psychological research on contact theory suggests that leaders must set appropriate conditions and manage social interactions between diverse groups so that the desired positive outcomes (e.g., reduced prejudice, positive relations, and increased collaboration) occur.[41] Specifically, leaders must:

a. Ensure that team members or groups are of equal status (or minimize differences in status). To do this, managers can carefully select the members and groups who will work together. They must also draw attention to the unique capabilities and experiences each member or group brings to the table.

b. Establish overarching or shared goals. This is critical because members and/or groups need to have a shared or common purpose; they should not be working at cross-purposes.

c. Encourage members or groups to work together on common goals. Leaders can enhance the likelihood of this happening by hosting introductory meetings, developing a shared mission statement, identifying specific goals, clarifying work rules and procedures, and providing feedback on how the larger group is working.

d. Encourage friendly, open interactions between members or groups. Even if participants are of different levels, keep these as democratic as possible.

e. Include informal personal encounters so that diverse members get to know one another in more depth, identify some common personal interests or values, and form cross-group friendships.[42]

Reflection:

Think about a situation in the past when a diverse team you led encountered relationship problems. Reviewing the conditions above, how could you have ensured an easier, more inclusive experience for the team?

Now think about a current or upcoming situation where you either have to work with a new, diverse team, or your team has to work with another group that is very different from your own. What are some things you can do to build a more inclusive and engaging work environment for everyone? Write down three or more ideas on how you can build inclusion.

_____

_____

_____

Put inclusion into practice by posing the same question to your team. Discuss and select the best ideas that would work for all of you.

Refer to Tool 5.3 for ideas to enhance your ability to listen to your people and relate with empathy. This is an activity to learn about the four levels of listening (from downloading to generative listening).

Refer also to Tool 5.4 for a checklist to increase your inclusiveness when planning and implementing activities with your team. This inclusive, change leadership checklist also provides a brief description of and reference to participative techniques such as World Café and Appreciative Inquiry to increase employee inclusion.

Takeaways

Employees are increasingly seeking a workplace where they feel included, yet research shows that only a small percentage of companies consider themselves truly inclusive. Here are some key takeaways from the chapter:

- Inclusion means that employees feel involved, valued and are fully integrated into their organizations.
- Underlying inclusion is trust, respect and fairness towards others.
- Inclusion is linked with fundamental human needs of belongingness and relatedness.
- Inclusion has been correlated with higher levels of employee engagement, team performance, and organizational productivity and profitability.
- Leaders play a major role in creating inclusive cultures that are characterized by a strong sense of psychological safety and interpersonal appreciation.
- We highlight four key inclusive leadership behaviors: being open, curious and adaptable; acting fairly; behaving authentically; and relating with empathy.

Tool 5.1. Video and Discussion: The Danger of a Single Story*

View a Ted Talk by Chimamanda Adichie to encourage participants to reflect on stereotyping and to expand their openness, awareness and appreciation for diversity.

The Ted Talk can be accessed at: https://www.ted.com/talks/chimamanda_adichie_the_danger_of_a_single_story

In this video, author Chimamanda Adichie relates her experiences as a Nigerian student coming to America and her experiences of stereotyping from others. The video is useful in helping leaders and managers reflect on the impact of their own experiences of stereotyping and of being stereotyped. It also provides an opportunity to be more aware of the risks related to having just a "single story" about a particular group or phenomenon. The reflection and discussion after the video will allow participants to recognize the kind of "single stories" we use everyday when working and relating with others.

After watching the video, reflect individually, and then preferably in small groups of other leaders and managers, on the following questions

1. After watching the video, what are your impressions?
2. What drew your attention? What seems to be especially important?
3. Working individually: Write down a story or two about:
   a. when you felt that somebody had "one story" about you

    b. if you have ever had "one story" about someone else

4. In small groups: Share stories with your colleagues. Listen for the emotions that are related to the stories and the consequences of these stories.

5. Large group summary:

    a. What are some ways to counteract "one story?"

    b. What are the implications for how we work with one another in our teams and the organization as a whole?

Tool 5.2. Discovering Multiple Intelligences*

This activity engages people to discover their multiple intelligences, shifting the focus from seeing deficits to seeing resources and strengths in others. It encourages the identification of each person's unique intelligence sets and the valuing of everybody's inherent worth.

Resources needed:
- Handout (Discovering my multiple intelligences; included after the instructions)
- Papers and pens; logical and mathematical puzzles; musical instruments; laptops with music and headset; mazes printed on paper and other games such as skipping rope, ping pong, bat with a ball; molding material (e.g., clay or Play Doh in several colors; objects from nature (e.g., wooden sticks, cones, stones, leaves, feathers); paper and glue

Exercise:

1. Make a presentation of the different types of intelligence, based on Howard Gardner's work, Frames of Mind (1983) and Intelligence Reframed (1999).
   - Spatial
   - Bodily-Kinesthetic
   - Linguistic
   - Logical-Mathematical
   - Musical
   - Interpersonal

- Intrapersonal
- Naturalistic
- Existential/Spiritual (newest type of intelligence, added later)

A useful website, Multiple Intelligences Oasis, https://www.multipleintelligencesoasis.org/, provides information about each type of intelligence. This website has a "quiz" or exercise that allows people to identify their multiple intelligences.

More information about multiple intelligences can also be obtained from Gardner's official website: https://howard-gardner.com

2. Provide a large space for participants to do activities for each of the nine intelligences. Give participants one hour to individually make use of different activities.

Here are some ideas for activities for each of the intelligences:
- Spatial: painting a picture on a specific topic; solving a puzzle; working on a "Tangram"
- Bodily-Kinesthetic: skipping with a skipping rope; bouncing a ball with a ping pong bat; juggling some objects
- Linguistic: writing a story based on a picture; writing a poem
- Logical-Mathematical: solving math puzzles; solving logical puzzle games
- Musical: playing musical instruments; clapping a rhythm; composing a song or tune; singing karaoke
- Interpersonal: teaching another person something; finding other people and doing something together with them (e.g., making music, playing a game)

- Intrapersonal: reflecting on your personal values and strengths; thinking about a moment in your life when you were truly yourself
- Naturalistic: creating an artistic object using natural objects such as sticks and cones; modeling a flower or animal with clay
- Existential/Spiritual: reflecting about the meaning of life, such as "If you could change one thing in the world, what would it be?"

3. Ask participants to make notes on a handout entitled "Discovering my multiple intelligences" after they have undertaken each activity. The handout asks them: How did you feel about the activity? Why? Do you think it indicates a strength? Do you think it reflects a unique intelligence or competence for you?

4. At the end of the hour, ask each participant to share with the larger group what they have discovered about themselves from the activities.

5. Practical application discussion for individuals and teams:
   - When you think of your tasks at work, do you find them to be a good fit for your type of your intelligence? Are they adequate for what you have to offer? What changes would you make?
   - What intelligences did we discover among each other in our team?
   - How do these intelligences affect how we think, work, interact and communicate?
   - What intelligences are we using and not using? What intelligences are we rewarding or recognizing?
   - How can we maximize the use of our team's intelligences?

Handout: Discovering my Multiple Intelligences

Intelligence	Activities Attempted	How did you feel about the activity? (Comments)	Does this activity reflect a strength, intelligence or competence for you? (1=Not a strength, 5=Clearly a strength)
1. Spatial			
2. Bodily-Kinesthetic			
3. Linguistic			
4. Logical-Mathematical			

5. Musical		
6. Interpersonal		
7. Intrapersonal		
8. Naturalistic		
9. Existential-Spiritual		

*Adapted from the "Inclusive Leadership Manual for Trainers". The manual was originally prepared by the School for Leaders Foundation, along with valuable contributions from the project partners, in particular from Irene Rojnik and Angelica Paci from alp activating leadership potential in Austria and from Michael Kraack, Heike Kraack-Tichy and Anna Sharapova from the EU-Fundraising Association e. V. in Germany. The manual can be downloaded and used free of charge by any company to improve their resilience under the terms of the Erasmus+ Programme. https://inclusiveleadership.eu/inclusive-leadership-manual-for-trainers/ The manual is subject to the license: **Creative Commons Attribution NoDerivatives Version 4.0** (CC-BY-ND, https://creative-commons.org/licenses/by-nd/4.0/legalcode). Reproduction is authorized provided that the source is acknowledged.

Tool 5.3. – Levels of Listening*

Inclusive leaders not only have a strong self-awareness and capacity for self-reflection and empathy for oneself, but they listen with genuine interest and value the contributions of others.

There are many levels of listening. This exercise is meant to increase leaders' and employees' awareness of how well and how deeply they listen to each other.

1. Divide your participants into teams of three people. Each member in the team selects a role: speaker, listener, and observer. Throughout the exercise, each person plays only this role. Each participant receives written instructions that the other members don't see.

    8 minutes (4 parts x 2 minutes)

    Guidelines for speakers:

    Task 1: Tell a short story about your professional work (2 minutes).
    Task 2: Tell a story about a trip that you've made (2 minutes).
    Task 3: Tell a story about a situation at work that provoked strong emotions in you (2 minutes).
    Task 4: Together with the listener, discuss ideas to do something good for the other team members; see if you can actually do something good during this time. (2 minutes).

Guidelines for listeners:

Task 1: Try to remember a similar situation as fast as possible and share your experience with the speaker.

Task 2: Try to capture key information in the speaker's story.

Task 3: Try to show the speaker that you are listening to him or her. Don't say anything.

Task 4: Together with the speakers, discuss ideas to do something good for the other team members; see if you can actually do something good during this time. (3 minutes).

Guidelines for observers:

During each of the tasks, observe and write down how the speakers and listeners behave, paying particular attention to body language, eye contact, the manner of speaker (including the words selected, intonation, voice volume, and what the speaker focuses on), as well as emotions. What differences can you spot during each of these tasks?

2. Reflection: After the fourth task, have each team (i.e., speaker, listener, observer) discuss the following questions:
   - What did you find out about each other?
   - Did you notice how the listener was listening in various ways in each of the conversations? If so, how? How did the speaker react, and how did this affect the conversation?
   - What feelings did the various conversations provoke in you?

3. Analysis and Generalization: Sum up the experience by introducing Otto Scharmer's theory of the four levels of listening.

You can show participants a video featuring Otto Scharmer: https://www.youtube.com/watch?v=eLfXpRkVZaI

In the video, Scharmer contends that lack of listening and connecting is the main source of failure among leaders and professionals in the workplace today.

Scharmer's four levels of listening:

- *Downloading* – "I know that already"; re-confirming what I already know. Downloading is listening from the assumption that you already know what is being said, and therefore only listening to confirm habitual judgments. You act from patterns you already know. (I-in-me).

- *Factual listening* – picking up new information. This is when you pay attention to what is new and different from what you already know. (I-in-it)

- *Empathic listening* – Seeing something through another person's eyes and forgetting your own agenda. This type of listening is when the focus is on the speaker, not the listener. The listener tries to experience what it is like to be in the speaker's shoes. (I-in-you).

- *Generative listening* – This deeper level of listening is when things slow down and inner wisdom is accessed through the conversation. In group dynamics, this is referred to as "synergy," when there is a unity and flow in the conversation between the speaker and listener, and something new, unique and good is created. (I-in the here and now).

4. Practical Application/Reflection:
   - To what extent (or at what level) do you typically listen to people at work?
   - What affects our capacity to listen deeply?
   - How can we strengthen our communication with others? What strategies can we use to listen better?

Tool 5.4. Checklist for Inclusive Change Leadership*

Inclusive leaders work collaboratively. They involve as many colleagues and teams as possible, creating a safe space where people can participate and feel a sense of belonging. The inclusive leader ensures that minorities (stakeholders who are both inside and outside the organization) are included and integrated so that their voices and interests are taken into account. The goal of the inclusive leader is a build a shared vision and to motivate the collaborative creation of a more inclusive and productive workplace.

We recommend leaders reflect on their current approach to planning and implementing activities, and consider adapting the behaviors in this checklist to enhance inclusion and collaboration with others.

- Focus on the strengths and talents of your team.

- Encourage your team members to identify their strengths and talents individually and to ensure that these are put to use appropriately.

- Create an atmosphere where your team feels secure, and every member is encouraged to play an active role.

- Encourage each team member to bring up concerns and discuss ideas beyond the scope of their own work responsibilities, so that the broader group benefits from their input.

- Ensure that your team members understand the boundaries within which they are allowed to innovate and the standards they must meet.

- Be sensitive that this shared approach does not harm individuals, groups or the surroundings. Review actions and ideas to prevent any harm to other stakeholders.

- When implementing ideas, be guided by a shared purpose that is clearly formulated and larger than the individual interests of the organization.

- Use collaborative forms of work, such as World Café and Appreciative Inquiry, when working with groups. We describe these briefly below:

  ▫ World Café: This is a technique of bringing large groups together to foster dialogue on issues and topics that are meaningful to them. The number of participants could vary from twelve to hundreds. Essentially participants sit in small tables (four to five people); these tables may be decorated with a tablecloth (hence "World Café") and paper for people to write and draw on. Participants at each table discuss questions such as "What opportunities can we see in this situation? What would it take to create change on this issue?[1]

  ▫ Participants get to move to other tables after twenty or thirty minutes, allowing them to have new conversations with new and diverse people, hence developing new relationships. One table member stays behind to host and relay key ideas from previous conversations.

The idea behind World Café is to engage participants on important issues through conversations, and to build on collective insights that emerge and drive action.

More information about World Café is available at: www. theworldcafe.com

☐ Appreciative Inquiry: This is an increasingly popular method of engaging teams and organizations in a process of positive exploration and creative dialogue. Instead of following the standard problem-solving approach of looking for what is wrong, or not working in the organization, then engaging in a causal analysis, solution generation and implementation, the appreciative inquiry method focuses participants on what is going well, what people value and are proud of, what their visions of the future are, and how they can create a future based on strengths, best practices, rewarding experiences, and successes.[2] Studies have shown that appreciative inquiry has been successful in creating an inclusive and hopeful environment that stimulates the generation of new ideas with groups being less bogged down by negativity and conflict.[3]

There is a worldwide portal on Appreciative Inquiry where resources and practical tools, such as interview guides and workshop designs, can be obtained: https:// appreciativeinquiry.champlain.edu/

[1] Brown, J. (2005, p. 173). The World Café: Shaping our future through conversation that matters. San Francisco, CA: Berrett-Koehler.

[2] Cooperrider, D. L. & Whitney, D. (2005). Appreciative inquiry: A positive revolution in change. San Francisco, CA: Barrett-Koehler.

[3] Anderson, D. L. (2017). Organization development. The process of leading organizational change (4th ed.). Thousand Oaks, CA: Sage.

*Adapted from the "Inclusive Leadership Manual for Trainers". The manual was originally prepared by the School for Leaders Foundation, along with valuable contributions from the project partners, in particular from Irene Rojnik and Angelica Paci from alp activating leadership potential in Austria and from Michael Kraack, Heike Kraack-Tichy and Anna Sharapova from the EU-Fundraising Association e. V. in Germany. The manual can be downloaded and used free of charge by any company to improve their resilience under the terms of the Erasmus+ Programme. https://inclusiveleadership.eu/inclusive-leadership-manual-for-trainers/ The manual is subject to the license: **Creative Commons Attribution NoDerivatives Version 4.0** (CC-BY-ND, https://creativecommons.org/licenses/by-nd/4.0/legalcode). Reproduction is authorized provided that the source is acknowledged.

Chapter 6

Relate with Authenticity and Emotional Intelligence

"A positive relationship is one in which there is a true sense of mutuality and relatedness such that people experience mutual giving and receiving, caring and safety in challenging times."
–Scott DeRue & Kristina Workman

If we want people to be more engaged, what can we do from a relationship perspective? How can we create better relationships? How can you promote positive relationships with your team members? In this chapter, we're focusing on relationships and how – by relating with authenticity and emotional intelligence – employee engagement and team success is enhanced. We'll look at the underpinnings of connection and authentic leadership. Although our emphasis is on the relationship between managers and team members, the concepts here can obviously be applied to other relationships at work, e.g., employees' relationships with each other, their relationships with other stakeholders and relationships with clients. (Also, see Chapter 1, which addresses appreciative and engaged communication.)

Reflection:

1. *How do you relate and make a connection with your team members?*
2. *Do your team members know how to work with you?*
3. *Do you check in frequently with your team members? How?*

What ideas do you have for enhancing your behavior in these three areas?

Relationship with Employees

• •

"If you don't have relationship, you start from zero each time."
–Kofi Annan

• •

There is a popular saying that employees leave their bosses, not their organizations. Relationships at work are a significant facet of employee engagement: some research has demonstrated a high correlation between a team member's relationship with his manager and his engagement.[1] More than 55% of respondents stated that their relationship with their immediate supervisor was very important.[2] Building effective relationships with employees is high on the list of leadership behaviors needed for engagement and success.[3] Some consider this relationship to be the most important one at every stage of the employee experience.[4]

Employee engagement is enhanced when your team members know you well, know what you stand for and trust that you will be honest with them. Fifty-five percent of employees who strongly agreed that they could talk with their manager about non-work-related issues were engaged, versus 8% who were engaged if they strongly disagreed. In addition, 54% of employees who strongly agreed that they are able to approach their leader with any kind of question were engaged; versus only 2% who were engaged when they strongly disagreed; and 65% of those who strongly disagreed were actively disengaged.[5] Engaging team leaders are caring, fair and honest.[6] Emotional connection on a personal level encourages increased pride and commitment, resulting in higher levels of engagement. This is especially true for Millennials.[7] Rather than a command and control boss, Millennials want a coach, someone who values them.[8] They want to be emotionally and behaviorally connected to their jobs.

Two critical aspects of relating successfully with your team members is to be authentic and to have high emotional intelligence. We'll address these two areas in the next sections.

Authentic leadership

• •

"... we need authentic leaders—people who own their mistakes, acknowledge their faults, and always put the interests of their organizations ahead of self-interests. Young leaders need role models whose actions provide guidance for their leadership."
–Bill George

• •

Take a moment to assess your authenticity by completing the survey below, using the scale:

Never (N), Rarely (R), Sometimes (S), Often (O) and Always (A).

At the bottom of the table, total the number of times you circle each letter. Consider your pattern:

- Which behaviors are you often or always doing? These indicate areas of strength for you.
- Which behaviors are you never or rarely doing? These suggest behaviors that you should try to do more frequently.

Rating	Authenticity
N R S O A	1. I "walk my talk."
N R S O A	2. I am clear about my values and standards.
N R S O A	3. My team members know how to work with me.
N R S O A	4. I explain the rationale for important decisions.
N R S O A	5. I ask for feedback on the impact of my behavior, style and approach.

Authentic leadership starts with the heart. Authentic leaders have integrity, are true to themselves and are genuine and transparent about their values, interests and preferences. They reveal some personal information about themselves, demonstrating some vulnerability. This openness helps to build stronger relationships with their team members.[9] Transparency is partially correlated with integrity, and followers who perceive their leader to be transparent are more engaged.[10] As well as being open, authentic leaders are genuinely interested in soliciting the input of employees. Because of this, team members view the manager as someone who is trustworthy.

Ultimately, trust is crucial to engagement. Authentic leaders are compassionate and focus on both performance results and engagement. They are credible, "walk their talk" and by so doing, build trust and meaningful connections with others. In organizations where less than 50% of leaders behaved in accordance with the company's values, only one third of the employees would recommend their organization to others as a good place to work. In addition, less than half of the team members were proud to work for their company.[11] Authentic leadership encourages employees to put in more effort at work – as a way of repaying their leaders – resulting in higher engagement and job satisfaction.[12]

Authentic leaders are self-aware – they know their strengths, are willing to admit their mistakes, and will work to overcome their weaknesses. They are continuously developing as they learn through their experiences and challenges. Gallup found that great leaders were analytical and objective in their decision-making.[13] This helps to build trust as employees understand that decisions are fair and made for the good of the department/ organization and all relevant information has been taken into consideration. In other words, the manager isn't playing favorites or putting her own interests first.

Authenticity and integrity are manifested through action. Team leaders in highly engaged teams are fair, honest, good role models and treat all team members fairly.[14]

Case Example – Authentic Leader[15]

An example of an authentic leader is Bill George – in fact, he wrote the book on it (literally! – "Authentic Leadership," 2003). Bill is currently a senior fellow at the Harvard Business School and serves on the board of directors at several large corporations. Earlier in his career, he was a senior executive at Honeywell and Litton Industries.

In 1989, he joined Medtronic, and during his tenure, he held the positions of president, CEO and Chairman of the Board. Bill says that he wasn't a natural born leader, but really learned his leadership skills during his time at Medtronic. Others on the senior management team had wanted the CEO position, and he had to ensure that he used his leadership skills to get them on board to support him.

Also, he was surprised at the ethical problems the organization had outside the USA – especially as the organization had such good values. He had to replace staff in several countries, including a senior executive that Bill had appointed (who was running a bribery fund). Bill had to admit he had made a mistake in appointing that person. Bill was shocked that the company's values weren't being adhered to, and that even some executives, who weren't unethical themselves, were tolerating this behavior in others. This is one of the reasons that Bill professes the crucial need for leaders in an organization to demonstrate its values and to be exemplary role models of those values. Towards the end of his time at Medtronic, he had to fire a CIO who had been at the company for just a few weeks. The

CIO was more interested in where his reserved parking space was rather than focusing on the goals of the organization!

Bill believes that you must be yourself to be an authentic leader, that everyone has leadership qualities and those qualities need to be developed. However, authenticity doesn't give leaders the permission to be "jerks" – to be rigid, rude, not adapting to changes – but it allows them to be themselves, while always striving to be an even better leader. Authentic leaders admit their mistakes and weaknesses and put the organization's interests before their own.

• •

"I had people trying to fix my weaknesses in previous jobs at Litton and Honeywell for twenty years. They were always unsuccessful because you couldn't fix them. I'm still impatient. I'm still too direct. I still lack tact. I still have all those weaknesses I've had all along. I hope I've moderated them a little bit, and they aren't quite as strong, but they're still there. They are part of who I am."
–Bill George

• •

See Tool 6.1 (an in-depth Authenticity Questionnaire) at the end of the chapter, so you can assess whether or not you're relating authentically with your team members.

Authentic leaders are self-aware, empathetic, and are also able to handle conflict situations effectively. We'll address these issues in the next section.

Emotional Intelligence

Before reading further, assess your emotional intelligence by completing the survey below, using the scale:

Never (N), Rarely (R), Sometimes (S), Often (O) and Always (A).

At the bottom of the table, total the number of times you circle each letter. Consider your pattern:

- Which behaviors are you often or always doing? These indicate areas of strength for you.
- Which behaviors are you never or rarely doing? These suggest behaviors that you should try to do more frequently.

Rating	Emotional Intelligence
N R S O A	1. I can accurately describe what I'm feeling.
N R S O A	2. I know the people/situations that anger or frustrate me.
N R S O A	3. I am able to admit my own mistakes.
N R S O A	4. I have effective strategies to help me when I'm feeling angry or out of control.
N R S O A	5. I find it easy to read the emotions of others.
N R S O A	6. I recognize how my behavior affects others.
N R S O A	7. I can express my needs respectfully, even when I'm angry.

N R S O A	8. I handle conflicts skillfully.

High levels of leader Emotional Intelligence (EQ) results in higher employee engagement.[16] EQ is a fundamental leadership skill – how do you manage yourself and your relationships? It is related to employee engagement in that managers who have higher EQ skills are more effective leaders, and effective management is essential for higher employee engagement. Leaders who have high EQ understand how they can build or deplete the autonomy, competence and relatedness (components of employee engagement) of their team members. On the other hand, leaders with lower EQ may not realize how they are draining their employees in these areas.

Higher EQ results in:

- Improved communication skills
- More productive relationships
- Increased collaboration and conflict management
- Enhanced thinking, problem-solving and decision-making
- Improved work performance and leadership potential

See Tool 6.2 – A more comprehensive Emotional Intelligence Self-Assessment.

Emotional intelligence (EQ) involves managing your own emotions and your relationships with others. According to Goleman, Boyatzis & McKee, it has four components (see diagram below): self-awareness, self-management, social awareness (empathy) and managing relationships.[17] Personal competence comprises the first two components – self-awareness (being able to recognize and identify your own emotions as they occur) and self-management (being able to control your emotions as they arise). Social competence includes social awareness (empathy – your ability to identify the emotions of others) and relationship management (being effective when relating with others, including communications skills, networking, collaboration and conflict management).

EQ Skill Model*

	Recognition – What I See	Regulation – What I Do
Personal Competence	*Self- Awareness* My ability to recognize my emotions and drives	*Self-Management* My ability to control or redirect my emotions and inclinations
Social Competence	*Social Awareness (Empathy)* My ability to identify the emotions and tendencies of others	*Relationship Management* My ability to manage my relationships with others

*Based on Goleman, Boyatzis & McKee's model[17]

Here's a quick review of the four EQ components with some ideas for enhancing each one.

Self-Awareness

Self-awareness is the foundational component of EQ and is a key feature of the authentic leader. If you aren't self-aware, you're probably – to some extent – closed off from your emotions and you may not notice the impact situations or other people have on you.

Ideas for enhancing self-awareness:

- Regularly tune in to your emotions (you can use the "Range of Emotions" – Tool 6.3 – to identify your feelings).
- Know your own emotional triggers. Keep a journal so you can record circumstances that trigger your emotions (an example is the SNAAP log – Tool 6.4 – and instructions for the log – Tool 6.5).
- Be aware of who and what pushes your buttons.
- Know your habits, strengths and weaknesses, and how you handle stress.
- Know your motivation.
- Know your values.
- Practice daily reflection.
- Practice regular mindfulness meditation.
- Review your responses to the self-awareness questions in the EQ survey (Section A of Tool 6.2). What are your strengths, and how could you enhance your self-awareness score?

Self-Management

If you're not able to manage your emotions and behavior, you'll be creating an unsafe volatile environment, which will diminish your trustworthiness (others don't know how you'll react), and you will probably create an atmosphere of non-approachability.

Ideas for enhancing self-management:

- Practice mindfulness techniques (e.g., meditation, deep breathing, counting to ten).
- Exercise – e.g., go out for a walk.
- Be compassionate with yourself.
- Take a break – ask to meet/discuss the matter later, so you have time to calm yourself down and gain control of your emotions.
- Use the SNAAP log (Tool 6.4 and instructions for the log – Tool 6.5) to review your reactions to situations and plan for future events.
- Be aware of your triggers, so you can plan ahead for your likely reactions.
- Use positive self talk.
- Recite self-calming statements.
- Review your responses to the self-management questions in the EQ survey (Section B of Tool 6.2). What are your strengths, and how could you enhance your self-management score?

Now, let us take a look at the social competency skills – empathy and relationship management.

Empathy (Social Awareness)

Empathy is the ability to understand or feel what another individual (or group) is experiencing – to be able to put yourself in their position. Research demonstrates that empathy is positively related to higher performance.[18]

Ideas for enhancing empathy:

- Put yourself in the other person's shoes – how do you see things from their perspective?
- Observe others – not just what they say, but how they say it, and note their body language.
- Cultivate curiosity and ask questions – learn about others.
- Strengthen your listening skills.
- Determine your biases and analyze their impact on others.
- Seek feedback from others.
- Review your responses to the empathy questions in the EQ survey (Section C of Tool 6.2). What are your strengths, and how could you enhance your empathy score?

Case Example – EQ Coaching

A coaching client had an issue in that his employees weren't participative, wouldn't initiate new ideas at team meetings and weren't very productive. The client's boss had spoken to him about the fact that he seemed to be fairly dictatorial in meetings, was easy to anger, and because of his "bullying" persona, team members were fearful, wouldn't volunteer their ideas, and were becoming less engaged. With this kind of leadership style, the client was informed that he probably wouldn't be considered for a promotion.

The client engaged a coach "on the side" – not wanting his boss to know about it. This client needed to improve his emotional intelligence. He didn't have high self-awareness, he wasn't able to manage his feelings, and he couldn't easily identify the effect he had on other people. By using the SNAAP log (Tool 6.4), the client was able to start sensing when he was getting heated (self-awareness) and was eventually able to take some deep breaths and stop himself from "flying off the handle" (self-management).

We reviewed the incidents in his log, and he began to recognize when he was just about to snap at someone. This was a step-by-step process – he caught himself at times, but not at other times. He continued with the SNAAP log, so he could analyze why he became emotional, and he was able to determine how he could more effectively handle a similar situation in the future. He also became more aware of how his outbursts affected everyone in meetings (social awareness/empathy), noticing how much more relaxed employees became as his angry retorts lessened. He realized the benefits of leading with higher emotional intelligence – his staff eventually stopped "walking on eggshells," were more participative in meetings, and their engagement and productivity increased. This change didn't happen overnight – it took over a year, but the client was eager to learn and willing to try new behaviors.

The nice thing is that it also benefitted the client at home as he treated his children differently too – instead of micro-managing how they did things (e.g., get dressed, brush their teeth), he gave them the leeway to do it their way as long as the end goal was achieved.

In addition, about six months later, during his performance review, his director mentioned that his behavior had improved tremendously, the productivity of his team had increased, and he was now being considered for a promotion.

Relationship Management

The foundation of effective relationship management is communication as this impacts all facets of relationship management: networking, collaboration, teambuilding and conflict management. This whole book focuses on your relationship with your team members. Thus far, we have already addressed: communications skills in Chapter 1; how you can nurture and support your employees in their career development in Chapter 2; and performance management and coaching skills in Chapter 4. Here, we'll focus on some strategies you can use to enhance your relationship with your employees (which will contribute to higher engagement).

Steps in effective relationship management:

1. Know your employees.
2. Have regular meetings with your employees.
3. Be an effective team leader.
4. Practice constructive conflict management.

1. Know Your Employees – Learn About Their Needs and What Is Important to Them:

   - Know the strengths of your direct reports (covered in Chapter 3)

- From your conversations with your direct reports, you know their needs and career aspirations. (In Chapter 2, we addressed nurturing / career development.)
- You also need to understand the style of those you work with. Use of an assessment such as the DiSC profile (which is widely used in the workplace) helps team members understand themselves and others, enhancing communication, relationships and productivity. Other instruments that are used in the workplace include: The Myers-Briggs assessment, True Colors, StrengthsFinder, the Big Five, the Predictive Index, the Hogan Personality Inventory, and various Emotional Intelligence assessments.

2. Have Regular Meetings with Your Employees:

Meetings are one way you can connect with your direct reports and build strong relationships. Do you have regular meetings with your employees? If you do, your direct reports are more likely to be engaged.[19] Engagement is at its highest when the meetings are held at least once a week. Some organizations have "asynchronous" meetings – i.e. they use emails, text, or other means of written communication. These "meetings" don't have to be long conversations, but these regular check-ins ensure that you:

- Keep the lines of communication open
- Are up-to-date on what's going on
- Get to know each of your team members as individuals
- Demonstrate to your employees that they matter and are valued
- Show your respect and support
- Promote trust
- Establish your approachability

Your meetings/check-ins can be short and simple and cover questions like:

1. How's everything going with you?
2. What do you think would make things better?
3. How can I support you?

Reflection:

Have you been meeting regularly with each of your direct reports? If not, plan now who you will meet with, when, and the agenda for the meeting.

---

3. Be an Effective Team Leader:

One way of promoting teamwork is addressed in Chapter 3 – having employees know their strengths and those of their colleagues to ensure that the unique talents of each individual are harnessed in pursuit of a common goal.

In addition:

- Clarify roles, responsibilities and expectations
- Create a team identity
- Build trust and inspire teamwork
- Facilitate and support team decisions
- Expand team capabilities by developing team members
- Capitalize on team strengths and differences
- Attend to the team's and organization's needs

4. Practice Constructive Conflict Management:

Whenever there is tension or conflict amongst your team members, it's important that you recognize the conflict (empathy/ social awareness) so you can do something about it, ensuring that your employees continue to be motivated and engaged. Engaged teams don't shy away from constructive debate and discussions to resolve issues. Ideally, your employees can handle the conflict themselves. (This was mentioned in Chapter 4.) However, if they aren't able to do that, then you need to address it.

<u>Steps for Managing Conflict Between Two Team Members:</u>

1. Describe the purpose of the conversation – state the issue. Be compassionate, clear and direct.
2. Explain the impact on you, the other team members, the project and the organization.
3. Ask each person to share their perspective and encourage active listening.
4. Ask questions / clarify – so you understand their perspectives; be curious. Show you've heard and understand them.
5. Identify and examine the roots of the conflict (some common causes are: miscommunications or differences in values, work styles, agendas or priorities).
6. Explore solutions – have each person identify how the situation could be changed; in collaboration, identify solutions both parties can support.
7. Agree to a plan and clarify steps for implementation.
8. Thank your employees for working together to resolve the conflict; confirm your confidence in – and commitment to – future effective communication.

9. Follow up on the plan.

Afterwards, reflect: What was effective? What could have been done differently?

Another idea for improving your relationship management skills is to review your responses to the relationship management questions in the EQ Assessment (Section D of Tool 6.2). What are your strengths, and how could you enhance your relationship management score?

This chapter has focused on you – the leader – and how you relate to your team members. As you are developing your employees and helping them to grow and progress, the concepts in this chapter are critical in their learning of leadership skills. How do you think your team members would respond to the Authenticity and Emotional Intelligence questionnaires? How can you help your team members to grow and develop in these two areas?

Takeaways

- Your relationship with your employees is critical for engagement.
- Authentic leadership is essential.
- High emotional intelligence is correlated with engagement.
- The components of emotional intelligence are self-awareness, self-management, empathy (social awareness) and relationship management.
- The steps in effective relationship management are: know your employees, have regular meetings, be an effective team leader, and practice constructive conflict management.

Tool 6.1: Authenticity Questionnaire

Questionnaire: Assess the extent to which you are relating authentically with your employees using the scale:

Never (N), Rarely (R), Sometimes (S), Often (O) and Always (A).

At the bottom of the table, total the number of times you circle each letter.

Consider your pattern:

Which behaviors are you often or always doing? These indicate areas of strength for you.

Which behaviors are you never or rarely doing? These suggest behaviors that you should try to do more frequently. Create a plan to improve in these areas.

N R S O A	1. I am a good role model.
N R S O A	2. I am ethical and fair with high performance standards.
N R S O A	3. I am clear about my values and standards.
N R S O A	4. My employees know how to work with me.

N R S O A	5. I "walk my talk" / keep my promises.
N R S O A	6. I "live" the organization's mission and values? (My actions support them).
N R S O A	7. I am approachable.
N R S O A	8. I am trustworthy.
N R S O A	9. I am able to control my feelings rather than being temperamental.
N R S O A	10. My team members feel "safe" working for me.
N R S O A	11. I know each person on my team personally.
N R S O A	12. I feel comfortable having a frank discussion with my team members. *
N R S O A	13. I am open about my strengths and weaknesses.
N R S O A	14. I demonstrate concern for my employees.
N R S O A	15. I make decisions analytically, based on performance (rather than politics).
N R S O A	16. I explain the rationale for important decisions.
N R S O A	17. I link my personal values (and those of employees) with goals, requests and action steps.

N R S O A	18. I ask for feedback on the impact of my behavior, style and approach.
N R S O A	19. I show I genuinely care about my team member's values and interests, making it a habit to ask frequently about their needs and personal situations.
N R S O A	20. I demonstrate a genuine interest in and respect of differences in other people, avoiding stereotypes or judgements.

(* Review "Challenging Conversations" in Chapter 4 if you need guidelines for handling candid discussions with an employee.)

Tool 6.2: Emotional Intelligence (EQ) Assessment

EQ is your ability to recognize and manage your emotions and the emotions of others.

Score each statement as honestly as possible, circling the appropriate number:

1 = Never   **2** = Rarely   **3** = Sometimes   **4** = Often   **5** = Always

SECTION A	
1 2 3 4 5	1. I can tell when my emotions are affecting my performance.
1 2 3 4 5	2. I know my values, strengths and weaknesses.
1 2 3 4 5	3. I learn from my experiences.
1 2 3 4 5	4. I can correctly identify the underlying reasons for my feelings.
1 2 3 4 5	5. I ask people to give me feedback.
1 2 3 4 5	6. I'm patient and calm in difficult situations.
1 2 3 4 5	7. I ask for help when I need it.
1 2 3 4 5	8. I can accurately describe what I'm feeling.
1 2 3 4 5	9. I know when the mood/attitude of others is affecting me.

1 2 3 4 5	10. I know the people/situations that anger/frustrate me.
	TOTAL
SECTION B	
1 2 3 4 5	1. I do not become defensive when criticized.
1 2 3 4 5	2. I can think clearly and stay focused and calm in difficult circumstances.
1 2 3 4 5	3. I usually or always meet commitments and keep promises.
1 2 3 4 5	4. I focus on the goal no matter what is going on around me.
1 2 3 4 5	5. I'm able to admit my mistakes.
1 2 3 4 5	6. I don't let my emotions rule my life.
1 2 3 4 5	7. I know how to express my feelings appropriately.
1 2 3 4 5	8. I handle setbacks effectively.
1 2 3 4 5	9. I take responsibility for my behaviors and actions.
1 2 3 4 5	10. I have strategies to help me when I'm feeling angry/out of control.
	TOTAL
SECTION C	
1 2 3 4 5	1. I find it easy to read others' emotions.
1 2 3 4 5	2. I generally know how my colleagues will react in specific situations.

1 2 3 4 5	3. I try to see things from another's perspective.
1 2 3 4 5	4. I'm attentive to the emotional cues of others.
1 2 3 4 5	5. I appreciate the differences in how people handle things.
1 2 3 4 5	6. I recognize how my behavior affects others.
1 2 3 4 5	7. I feel compassion when I see others having a difficult time.
1 2 3 4 5	8. People tell me I'm a good listener.
1 2 3 4 5	9. I often observe people to see if there's a correlation between what they're saying, how they say it, and their body language.
1 2 3 4 5	10. I relate well with each of my colleagues.
	TOTAL
SECTION D	
1 2 3 4 5	1. I easily build rapport with colleagues and others.
1 2 3 4 5	2. I achieve win-win outcomes.
1 2 3 4 5	3. I can express my needs respectfully – even when I'm angry.
1 2 3 4 5	4. I relate well to people of different backgrounds.
1 2 3 4 5	5. I am able to give constructive feedback to others.
1 2 3 4 5	6. I am connected to a wide network of people
1 2 3 4 5	7. I am skillful at handling conflicts.

1 2 3 4 5	8. I'm an effective team player.
1 2 3 4 5	9. I am open to – and seek – feedback from others.
1 2 3 4 5	10. I show my appreciation to others.
	TOTAL

Capture your Scores and Calculate Your Overall EQ:

Section A	Self-Awareness	
Section B	Self-Management	
Section C	Empathy (Social Awareness)	
Section D	Relationship Management	
	Add the numbers:	
	Divide by 4	
	Overall EQ:	

What Your Scores Mean

31 or above	Above average – you can use this skill to maximize your success
30	Average – it could be a strength, with a little improvement
29 or below	Below average – this skill needs some work

Tool 6.3: Range of Emotions

	Happy	Sad	Angry	Confused	Hurt	Scared	Weak	Strong
Strong	Amazed Ecstatic Elated Enthusiastic Excited Exhilarated Inspired Jubilant Overjoyed Thrilled Uplifted	Crushed Defeated Dejected Depressed Devastated Dismal Empty Gloomy Heartbroken Hopeless Miserable	Appalled Enraged Fuming Furious Hostile Incensed Livid Mad Seething Vengeful	Bewildered Confounded Dazed Desperate Disoriented Lost Mystified Rattled Torn Trapped	Anguished Crushed Degraded Devastated Heartbroken Humiliated Maligned Punished Rejected Ridiculed Wounded	Afraid Alarmed Distraught Frightened Horrified Panicked Paralyzed Shocked Terrified Tormented	Beaten Drained Exhausted Helpless Hopeless Impotent Incapable Inferior Overwhelmed Small Useless	Assertive Courageous Determined Driven Dynamic Engaged Forceful Potent Proud Resolute Tenacious
Medium	Cheerful Content Delighted Fulfilled Glad Hopeful Jovial Warm	Disappointed Discouraged Disturbed Downcast Drained Fed up Tearful	Aggravated Annoyed Frustrated Offended Peeved Resentful Unsettled Upset	Ambivalent Disconcerted Disturbed Dubious Hesitant Mixed up Troubled Uncertain	Belittled Criticized Devalued Discredited Distressed Mistreated Resentful	Anxious Guarded Insecure Skittish Startled Unnerved Wary	Defensive Inadequate Insecure Lazy Listless Rundown Shaky	Capable Confident Energetic Persuasive Positive Safe Secure
Mild	Comfortable Fine Pleased Relaxed Satisfied	Blue Glum Somber Subdued Unhappy	Displeased Irked Irritated Resentful Unsettled	Bothered Puzzled Uncomfortable Undecided Unsure	Let down Miffed Neglected Rueful Sensitive	Apprehensive Cautious Uneasy Watchful Worried	Lethargic Shy Tired Unsatisfied Unsure	Ready Solid Steady Sure

Tool 6.4: EQ SNAAP© LOG

Complete this log as soon as possible after the event when you have experienced an incident in which you felt you were out of control

Date and Time	Incident (Describe briefly)	Sense (What did you physically feel?)	Name the emotion	Assign Cause (Trigger – what specifically caused the emotion?)	Appreciate (Accept and own your feeling/s.)	Plan (How to handle this feeling/situation in the future?)

Tool 6.5: EQ SNAAP© LOG – Explanation

The EQ SNAAP Log can be used to enhance both self-awareness and self-management.

As an awareness practice, use EQ SNAAP to accurately describe your current emotional status and clarify your motives and subsequent actions.

As a strategy for self-management, by identifying and owning your feelings, you are more likely to be able to control your feelings in the future. The "Plan" piece enables you to handle future similar situations more effectively.

S **SENSE**
What physical sensations did you feel in your body? (E.g., clenched fists or jaw, heat in the body-sweating/flushed cheeks, increased heart rate, increased rate of breathing, tightness in the belly, change in muscle tension, clammy hands, tight throat, etc.)

N **NAME**
Name the emotion – happy, sad, angry, afraid, etc., (see the "Range of Emotions" tool to help you differentiate the level of your emotion). The more accurately you can name the emotion, the more control you will have.

A **ASSIGN CAUSE**

Can you determine what triggered the emotion? Even though a current specific event seems to be the reason, there might be previous events that contributed to this emotion or to the intensity of the emotion.

A **APPRECIATE**

Appreciate and accept the emotion with compassion – the emotion itself is neither good nor bad but an inherent quality of being human. Own your feeling, without judging yourself.

P **PLAN**

How could you handle this emotion in this kind of situation in the future? Which coping strategies could you use?

Chapter 7

Empower Your Team to Succeed

The best executive is the one who has sense enough to pick good men to do what he wants done, and self-restraint enough to keep from meddling with them while they do it.
– Theodore Roosevelt

Are you an Empowering Leader?

Before we begin our discussion of empowerment, take a moment to assess the extent to which you are an empowering leader by completing the survey below, using the scale:

Never (N), Rarely (R), Sometimes (S), Often (O) and Always (A).

At the bottom of the table, total the number of times you circle each letter. Consider your pattern:

- Which behaviors are you often or always doing? These indicate areas of strength for you.
- Which behaviors are you never or rarely doing? These suggest behaviors that you should try to do more frequently.

Rating	Empowering Leadership
N R S O A	1. I ensure that my team members have the requisite training to perform their jobs well.
N R S O A	2. I give my team members access to all the information they need to make key decisions at work
N R S O A	3. I give my team members the freedom to decide how to go about their work, so long as it is aligned with team and organizational objectives.
N R S O A	4. I encourage my team members to feel a strong sense of responsibility for the outcomes of their work.
N R S O A	5. I support my team members on decisions they make on the job.
N R S O A	6. I coach my team members rather than tell them what to do.

To empower means to grant authority to another individual to think, make decisions, and act on their own in order to accomplish a particular task. For leaders and managers like you, what lies beneath the act of empowerment is the belief that your team is ready, willing and able to make autonomous choices, perform at a high level, and meet specific objectives. You trust your people and are confident that they will be able to get things done by leveraging various sources of power and influence within the organization.

The importance of autonomy and empowerment cannot be understated in today's world. Research on Millennials indicates that this generation wishes for their views to be considered before key decisions are made, whether these decisions pertain to climate change, world conflict, or other socio-political issues.[1]

Within the workplace, Millennials seek to be empowered and aspire to become leaders who can empower others. They dislike drone-like work and conformity, not because they are "entitled" but because they are in search of greater purpose and meaning.[2]

A recent Millennial Leadership study found that almost fifty percent of Millennials define leadership as "empowering others to succeed." Not surprisingly, most Millennials indicated a preference for working for companies with fewer management layers. Millennials acknowledge the importance of building relationships. They seek to be transformational leaders who can inspire their followers to be part of meaningful decisions and solutions that can impact their world.[3]

In this chapter, we will first seek to deepen our understanding of empowerment and why it is an important ingredient in fostering individual and team engagement, and performance. Then, we will discuss different sources of power that employees can personally harness within the organization. We will discuss what it means for employees to be ready, willing, and able to be empowered. We will identify empowering leader behaviors as well as characteristics associated with empowering organizations. Throughout the chapter, we include practical ideas to help managers assess, prepare, encourage and support successful empowerment and engagement in the workplace.

The Concept of Empowerment

It doesn't make sense to hire smart people and then tell them what to do; we hire smart people so they can tell us what to do.
— Steve Jobs

The concept of empowerment is quite complex and can be viewed in multiple ways.

First, empowerment can be defined as the employee's psychological experience of "being in power," of being able to mobilize resources and significantly influence work or organizational outcomes by themselves.[4] From a practical perspective, empowerment is akin to allowing employees to act like "entrepreneurial owners." For example, Ian Clough, CEO of DHL Express U.S. describes empowerment in terms of encouraging employees to be "entrepreneurs" within their own organization. [5] By connecting employees so strongly to the mission and vision of the organization, they feel personally invested in it. Furthermore, by giving employees the power to decide what would support the best interests of the company, they are most likely to participate in the decision-making process as responsibly as possible.

Second, empowerment can be viewed from your own mindset (the leader's mindset). As mentioned in our introductory chapter , empowerment requires a distinct leadership mind shift, moving away from what Douglas McGregor calls a Theory X assumption that employees are by nature lazy and need to be micromanaged, to a Theory Y assumption that employees are naturally motivated to grow and take on responsibility by themselves.[6] If you are a Theory Y empowering leader, your job would be to clarify the goals, set the stage, and then, per Teddy Roosevelt's statement above, stop meddling and get out of the way as your employees go about their jobs.

Building on this, the third way of viewing empowerment is focusing on the specific actions and practices of leaders to promote the sense of empowerment among individuals and teams as well as to create an empowering organizational culture.[7]

Case Example – Zappos

An excellent contemporary example of empowerment is Zappos, the online shoe retailer. The first of Zappos' core values is "to deliver WOW through service." Its vision is to be the online service leader with the best selection and best service for shoes and other related products.

In pursuit of this, Zappos felt that the traditional hierarchy was very inefficient for communication, problem solving, customer service, and innovation. Thus, at the end of 2014, the company consciously did away with its hierarchical structure, eliminating management positions and erasing the typical silos between merchandising, finance, IT, and other departments. Instead. Zappos has created self-managing, self-organizing business-centric groups made up of empowered employees who are responsible for multiple specific roles and for working closely with their peers and customers to support the higher goals of the organization.[8] Within this "holacracy" (self-managing organization), power is distributed, employees and employee groups set up their own structures and processes, and make decisions about virtually everything including who to hire and fire, how to distribute roles and responsibilities, how to solve problems, which teams or task forces should be formed and so on.

CEO Tony Hsieh explains that this does not mean the absence of management, in terms of setting direction, planning, controlling, evaluating, etc. Rather, these management roles have been spread widely among empowered employees. According to Hsieh, "it can be argued that there is more management and leadership happening at any time in self-managing organizations despite, or rather precisely because of, the absence of fulltime managers." [9]

For most of us, Zappos' demonstration of empowerment might be quite extreme, and, indeed, the company may not be for everyone. Yet it would be difficult to argue against Zappos' success as well as the high level of engagement among its employees. In fact, Zappos has an engagement department called P.E.A.C.E. (Programs, Events, Activities, Charity and Engagement) that administers various programs like M.O.M. (to recognize mentors), Hero/Sidekick Awards (to recognize peers), Wishez (to enable employees to make and grant wishes), and various civic and charitable activities around the Las Vegas area where the company is located. In 2015, Zappos was rated as #86 of the 100 Best Companies to work for by Fortune Magazine, and as of 2018, the company exceeded $1 billion in annual revenues from the sale of shoes, clothing and accessories. [10]

Having read the example of Zappos', let's now assess your baseline of empowerment in your organization. The introductory questions in this chapter asked you to think about what you do to empower employees. Now, we encourage you to take the perspective of an employee and think about your own experience of being empowered (or not) in your organization.

Reflection:

On a scale of 1 to 10 (1= not empowered at all and 10 = highly empowered), how empowered do *you* feel in your own organization?

What factors contribute to your current level of empowerment (or disempowerment)?

How does your sense of empowerment (or disempowerment) affect your personal engagement and performance at work?

Specifically, what do your leaders do and not do that contribute to this level of empowerment (or disempowerment)?

Empowerment and Engagement

To understand how empowerment and engagement are related, let us closely examine the core dimensions of psychological empowerment.[11] These are:

- Self-determination (the ability to choose and make decisions, i.e., to be autonomous)
- Self-efficacy (the certainty about your own skills and abilities)
- Personal consequence (the power to have a positive and significant effect on others)

- Meaning (the importance of the purpose or goals of your work)
- Trust (the belief in the reliability of others, such as your manager or peers)

These five empowerment dimensions overlap with Kahn's original notion about what drives work engagement.[12] As discussed in Chapter 1, Kahn found that work engagement is most likely to occur when people have a sense of psychological safety, personal availability (energy and resources) and meaningful work. Thus, for people to be both empowered AND engaged in their work, they must have the freedom and authority to determine their own actions (without fear of reprisal), they must be confident in their abilities and have the trust and support of their managers and peers and they must be doing something that is important and personally meaningful. (Refer to Figure 7.1 for linkages between empowerment and engagement.)

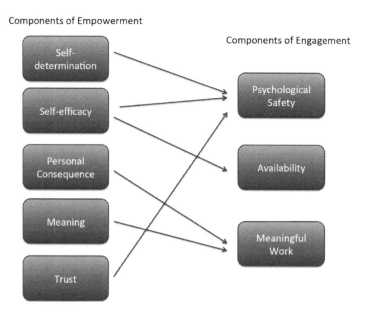

Figure 7.1. Links between Empowerment and Engagement

The most distinctive aspect of empowerment is self-determination, also referred to by others as autonomy. Research on self-determination theory has shown that human beings are more strongly motivated by intrinsic desires for personal control, growth and fulfillment.[13] Intrinsic factors such as the challenge of the task itself, and the creative anticipation and gratification of being able to control how to accomplish one's work, are more likely to engage people and generate longer-lasting motivation than extrinsic factors like monetary incentives. (Refer to selfdeterminationtheory.org, for more research and resources on intrinsic motivation and self-determination).

Empowerment involves allowing one's employees to select what they are doing and how they are doing it. They must have the power to make choices – to put their personal stamp on their endeavors. This can only occur successfully in a psychologically safe environment where they feel trusted and supported. By having the autonomy to create something that they are an important part of, they can harness and challenge more of themselves.

From an empowerment perspective, some of the worst things that could happen to people would be helplessness in determining their fate, and alienation (or disconnection) from the purpose of their work and from the camaraderie of others. These are among the top reasons why employees leave their jobs. The importance of empowerment as a driver of employee engagement has been consistently established in engagement research.

For example, Google conducted some very interesting extensive research to determine whether the quality of managers really matters to employees, and if so, how.[14] They found that excellent managers are primarily great coaches and excellent at empowering their teams. Specific examples of Google managers' empowering behaviors included listening to employees' ideas with respect, giving people space to act on their own while being available for advice, and advocating for their employees to the rest of the organization.

Empowerment and Performance

Cynical manager question: *Does empowerment merely make people feel good or is it significantly related to specific business outcomes?*

There is actually substantial, empirical evidence that empowerment predicts not just employee engagement but individual and team performance. For instance, one study reported that empowerment within municipal teams is associated with higher team performance. Four aspects of individual empowerment (autonomy, responsibility, creativity and information) contributed significantly to team performance.[15]

A meta-analytic review conducted across 142 research articles provides even more powerful evidence of the positive effects of empowerment. This review found that psychological empowerment is positively associated with individual job satisfaction, organizational commitment, and task and contextual performance, and negatively associated with employee strain and turnover intent. Additionally, team empowerment is linked directly with team performance.[16] The authors reported four factors to be significant antecedents (predictors) of psychological empowerment. These factors are:

1. High-performance managerial practices (e.g., information sharing, decentralization, training, employee participation in decision-making, and contingent rewards);
2. Socio-political support (e.g., establishing a supportive climate; building trust between leaders and employees);

3. Leadership (e.g., supportiveness; role modeling; feedback and coaching);

4. Work design characteristics (e.g., providing challenging tasks; task significance; autonomy; allowing employees to see the results of their work)

A field study examined levels of empowerment within 111 teams in four organizations. Findings revealed that the more empowered teams were more proactive and productive compared to the less empowered teams. Members of the more empowered teams had higher job satisfaction as well as team and organizational commitment. Four factors were found to contribute to team empowerment: leader behaviors, levels of responsibilities given to the teams, HR policies, and the social structures of the teams.[17]

Finally, a 2018 meta-analysis of 105 field experiments of leaders empowering employees showed that empowering leaders tended to be trusted more by their followers compared to leaders who were not empowering. Moreover, empowering leaders saw greater levels of employee creativity and citizenship behavior within their organizations.[18]

These research studies suggest that empowerment can, in fact, have a "powerful" impact on employees, teams and organizations, but for this to happen, there must be a confluence of multiple drivers. That is, employees and teams must be ready, willing and able; leaders must know how to facilitate empowerment among individual employees and teams; and the organizations must have the resources, systems and structures to support empowerment.

Exercise: How can leaders prepare for empowerment within their teams and organizations? What are its risks and benefits? (Tool 7.1 provides key questions for you and your colleagues to consider in the preparation process.)

DEEPER DIVE

Leveraging Sources of Power

Power is at the heart of the term "empowerment." Power is the ability to influence others toward the accomplishment of a goal. Empowered employees now have more opportunities to exert power and influence in various ways. Hence, it would be useful for managers, as well as employees, to understand and leverage different sources of power. In what different ways can you influence others, especially if you are not the boss? What are the options for getting things done, and are certain options better than others?

Some sources of an employee's power are formal, based on one's position in the organization. These are sometimes referred to as "hard" bases of power. For example, having a title of "Chief Operating Officer" confers legitimate power, such that lower-ranked employees feel obliged to follow the COO's demands or requests. Higher-ranking managers are able to administer rewards (e.g., bonuses) for good behavior; they may also coerce or pressure people to act in certain ways due to threat of punishment.

Other sources of power are more informal and related to people's characteristics. These are sometimes referred to as "soft" bases of power. For example, people tend to listen to employees who are recognized "experts" in a specific domain. Or, they may look up to certain people who are likable and charismatic, regardless of their rank in the organization. (This is called referent power). People can also gain power and influence by being "in the know" (i.e., having access to important news and information). In today's high-tech social-media environment, being highly connected to others, especially individuals and groups that matter to the employee, represents a tremendous source of power. This is true, not just for Millennials but all age groups. One just needs to look at the power of Twitter or Facebook and how certain leaders, celebrities or even regular folks are able to reach and influence thousands of followers. The idea of being "connected" to an important person, being able to exchange ideas or feedback in a highly visible and diverse forum, and potentially building one's own image, is attractive and influential to many people. Nowadays, many organizations employ electronic platforms like Slack, Samepage and Trello, where employees can communicate and share information and ideas online as well as initiate and collaborate on various projects using a variety of apps.

The key takeaway here is that while all sources of power have their uses, soft bases of power have been found to be more effective in influencing people than the hard bases of power. This is akin to the pull versus push mechanism, or the idea of free choice versus conformity. There has been very interesting management research showing that reward and coercion typically lead to compliance.[19] People obey mainly because of the consequences-even though their hearts and minds are not necessarily in the work.

On the other hand, using softer bases of power like expert or referent power leads to greater employee commitment and engagement to the manager's cause. People want to be inspired; they want to feel confident about their manager's expertise and access to critical information; and they want to feel a powerful sense of connection with others. By utilizing informal and personal sources of power, managers will be more likely to empower their own people. Empowered employees are also more likely to utilize informal and personal sources of power as they take on more responsibilities in their organizations. Interestingly, new research demonstrates that informal sources of power are linked with more innovative company cultures.[20]

Exercise: Do you know what sources of power you typically utilize as a leader? Tool 7.2 is a short self-assessment. After completing it, use the guide questions to reflect on your findings.

Understanding and Ensuring Readiness for Empowerment

Empowerment can be a terrifying concept for managers. So, before we summarize empowerment behaviors, let us be clear about the scope of empowerment. Empowerment does not mean, "simply letting go" or abdicating responsibility.[21] Neither does empowerment mean a free-for-all for employees, with no clarification of expectations or accountability.

Skillful empowerment involves having the leader first assess the readiness of individual employees as well as the readiness of the team and organization.

The following is a set of questions that managers can use to diagnose whether one's employees and environment are ready and/or suited for empowerment. (Note: If many of these conditions are not satisfied, efforts to empower employees will simply lead to frustration, disengagement and disillusionment.) These questions can also provide managers' guidelines about what needs to be created in their organizations to support empowerment on a system-wide basis.

At the employee level:

- Are your employees *ready* for empowerment? That is, are they independent, capable, self-monitoring and disciplined?
- Are they *willing* to be empowered? Are they interested in challenge, growth and development?
- Do they have the *ability* to be empowered? Do they have necessary (even superior) information and expertise? Might they have even more information or expertise than the manager?

Case Example – Valve

The video gaming company called Valve represents an example where careful employee selection provides a foundation for a culture of empowerment. Founded by former Microsoft employees, Valve is the maker of the popular science fiction first-person-shooter video game Half-Life and the digital distribution network Steam.

The company places a premium in selecting the most talented employees. As explained in Valve's handbook, "When you're an entertainment company that's spent the last decade going out of its way to recruit the most intelligent, innovative, talented people on Earth, telling them to sit at a desk and do what they're told obliterates 99 percent of their value." The company eschews the organizational hierarchy in favor of manager-free teams, allowing employees to decide which projects they wish to work on, and acknowledging their freedom to fail in the pursuit of greatness.[22]

In thinking about empowerment at the individual employee level, a key role that the leader should play is that of **talent manager**. Leaders need to recruit and select employees carefully to ensure they have the desired knowledge, skills, ability and attitudes to support empowered work. They also need to ensure that training is in place to maximize employees' opportunities to work autonomously and participate in decision-making. Training would include not just what they need for their jobs, but a broader understanding of the landscape in which they work.

For example, when on-boarding new employees (regardless of role), invest time in getting them to understand the organization's vision and mission, the types of products and services offered, how the organization is structured, who the key leaders are, which internal and external groups they will be interacting with the most, and where to find information about procedures, policies, etc. Showing them the big picture and where they fit in will enable them to be empowered and allow them to contribute more effectively to team and organizational improvement discussions.

At the team level:

- Are team members committed to the goals of the team and the organization as a whole?
- Do they know their roles and responsibilities?
- Are they supportive of each other?
- Do employees have access to information and feedback about their performance?
- Do they have a strong sense of individual and mutual accountability?

DEEPER DIVE

Creating a Results-oriented Work Environment (ROWE):
Focusing on the ends rather than the means

In the last several years, a practice called Results-oriented Work Environment (ROWE) has gained some popularity. ROWE was initially introduced at Best Buy in 2003 by two employees Jody Thompson and Cali Ressler who wanted to find a better way of managing knowledge workers. The essence of ROWE is the focus on setting and working toward performance goals (i.e., being outcome-driven rather than being handcuffed to the clock, or procedurally-bound). Employees could work wherever they wanted however they wanted, and for as long or short as they wanted, so long as they met individual and team goals. In this system, Best Buy employees were empowered to search for innovative ways to work together effectively and efficiently, often leading to large increases in productivity as well as employee satisfaction. Unfortunately, ROWE was discontinued in Best Buy 2012 when a new CEO took over the company.

Nevertheless, ROWE is being practiced by other organizations such as the Gap Outlet, Yum Brands (a national chain of restaurants), and J.A. Counter & Associates (an investment and insurance company). These companies have reported positive results including improved employee morale, cost savings, and increased productivity.

It must be noted that ROWE is more appropriate for knowledge-based industries where there is room for flexibility in both work time, place and process. It is not recommended for jobs or industries like emergency medical services where people need to be physically present at specific times and settings.[23]

A recent Global Talent Trends Survey by Mercer indicated that fifty-one percent of employees wish their companies offered more flexible work options, and more than eighty percent of working parents indicated that work flexibility and work-life balance were the two most important factors in a job for them.[24] Nevertheless, implementing work-flexibility programs like ROWE can be challenging. Some research suggests that people tend to work more under flexible work systems compared to standard 9-5 schedules, and that their work efforts spill over into personal and family time.[25] There are also fears (especially from males) that their careers could be impacted by using flexible work arrangements.[26] Clearly, there is room for leaders and organizations to allay such concerns, be role models, provide guidance, support and regular feedback to employees, and develop systems that track and reward work outputs (rather than work time).

In thinking about empowerment at the team level, a key role that the leader could play is that of **coach.** Coaching is discussed in more detail in Ch. 4. True empowerment lies in not micromanaging employees and teams but in facilitating and guiding them to achieve work goals. For example, Adobe is well known for fostering creativity in the digital world. Its leaders provide employees with very clear expectations and responsibilities; then they get out of the way to allow freedom and flexibility.[27] The company even created a tongue-in-cheek video called "The Hovering Art Director" to illustrate the pitfalls of micromanagement.[28]

At the organizational level:

- Does your company have values and norms that support individual and team empowerment?
- Is the organizational structure relatively flat, flexible and team-based?
- Does the culture support creativity and innovation at the organizational level as well as personal and career growth at the individual level?
- Are the systems and processes set up to quickly and easily provide and share information within and across groups inside and outside of the organization?
- Do employees have "skin" in the game? That is, are there rewards and recognition systems set up so that employees can equitably share in the fruits of their labor?

Case Example – Semco

An example of an organization that has done a wonderful job of setting up systems of empowerment is Semco[29]

In the early 1990's, Ricardo Semler had just taken over leadership of a Brazilian manufacturing company from his father during a time of major socio-economic bedlam and many businesses were going bankrupt. In his efforts to keep the business going and avoid mass layoffs, he consulted with his employees. They proposed a thirty percent pay cut for employees and a forty percent pay cut for managers for a set period of time in exchange for much greater percentage of profit sharing. Employees were energized to participate in decision-making and began acting more like "owners", wanting to know more about operations, finances and results; they also began undertaking more work on their own. As the company stabilized, Semco experimented with radical initiatives such as setting up a center of innovation to allow their engineers to create new products, improve old ones and think of new lines of business. Engineers' guaranteed salaries went down but they received a greater share of the proceeds of their inventions, and they were even allowed to offer consulting services to the public.

Ricardo Semler allowed employees to define how they wanted to work with the company, either as full-time or part-time employees, contractual employees, or even entrepreneurs, running their own satellite companies (with some initial support from the company). The company invested in educating its employees in business principles, quality and efficiency;

it also operated with an extraordinary level of transparency, with all its meetings and company books open to employees.

Employees could set their own work schedules; they even set their own salaries, under the assumption that peers and the free market would control what was ultimately acceptable. Semco's different business divisions utilized free- market principles to decide whether to fulfill production contracts using the services of internal groups or external companies. This forced internal groups to operate at the highest level of quality, efficiency and profitability. Semco's organizational structure was much flatter with only three levels: associates, partners (heads of divisions) and counselors. Interestingly, at the top level, there was not one but six counselors who take turns acting as CEO (every 6 months). The shorter leadership tenures forced the CEO's not to postpone difficult decisions and encouraged the counselors to inform each other constantly and share responsibility, symbolizing a model of participation and collective leadership.

Two memorable quotes from Semler summarize his philosophy of empowerment:

"We use minimal hierarchies, ad hoc structures, self-control and the discipline of our own community marketplace of jobs and responsibilities to achieve high quality, on time performance." (Semler,1994)

"Participation gives people control of their work, profit sharing gives them a reason to do it better, and information tells them what's working and what isn't." (Semler, 1989)

Semco continues to be a successful organization not only in Brazil but around the world. In its current form, Semco Partners is an active portfolio business working with foreign companies such as H&R Block, Cushman & Wakefield, and Pitney Bowers that wish to expand their businesses in Brazil. It continues its shared leadership structure with six partners who have worked together over several years.[30]

In keeping with his revolutionary philosophy, Ricardo Semler recently established a new type of school in Brazil (The Lumiar Schools) where students are the center of the learning, not the teachers. Students are allowed, within certain boundaries, to choose the subjects they wish to learn, and they vote as a group on learning tasks and activities. The teachers are organized as "tutors" who map out the development of each student, and "masters" who have both expertise and passion in diverse areas. Subjects are taught creatively within the sphere of students' current interests. For example, during World Cup season, various courses such as mathematics, history and health science were taught within an "international-soccer" framework.[31] While it is too early to assess the effectiveness of this radical educational style, Semler pushes us all to challenge the boundaries of leading, teaching and working.

In thinking about empowerment at the organizational level, a key role that the leader should play is that of **organizational architect**. As can be seen from the Semco example above, it can be argued that Ricardo Semler was not a laissez-faire leader who simply gave up the reins to his employees. Instead he created an invisible, yet powerful, structure – an environment within which people could have more control over their work and be innovative while maximizing their interests and that of the organization.

Empowering Manager Behaviors

Several authors have conducted survey and interview studies to identify different categories of empowering manager behaviors.[32] Moreover, the quantitative studies described in the earlier section outlined several antecedents of psychological empowerment. We have distilled these findings into three sets of empowering managerial behaviors:

1. **Information Sharing** – Managers who empower employees are constantly providing information about the team and company direction, goals and priorities. They trust their employees and strive to be open and transparent about both success and failure. Because employee involvement and commitment are important to them, they discuss the rationale for key decisions, policies and procedures, and share new developments in the organization, the industry and the environment. Empowering managers provide employees with the information and tools that enable their people to make great decisions, facilitate goal accomplishment, and monitor their own progress.

2. **Autonomy and Participation** – Empowering managers foster autonomy and encourage employee input in decision-making. They do not micro-manage; they believe the best decisions are often those made by capable employees at the front lines. They do not hesitate to share leadership

and continually demonstrate confidence, appreciation and respect for their valued employees. Empowering managers allow employees to set their own goals as well as their team's goals with the confidence that empowered employees seek to stretch and grow rather than plan conservatively. Empowering managers seek to eliminate bureaucratic constraints to speed up work and enhance flexibility and quality. They also look for ways to facilitate cross-level and cross-group interaction and cooperation.

3. **Feedback and Support** – Effective empowering managers constantly provide concrete and constructive feedback to facilitate their employees' success. They partner with their employees to think through and find solutions to challenges. They are great coaches who help their employees identify where they can best contribute and encourage them to be innovative and self-reliant. They set high standards for performance, but at the same time, provide a safe environment in which to try new ideas and behaviors. They serve as good advocates for their people, especially upwards and across the organization. They support their people through training, coaching, resources, feedback, rewards and recognition, partnerships with other groups, and so forth. For more discussion about performance management and engagement, refer to Chapter 4.

These three sets of behaviors, working in tandem, lead to empowered employees who are ready, willing and able (RWA) to engage and perform.

Refer also to Tool 7.3 for "Empowerment Do's and Don'ts".

Reflection:

Which of the empowering behaviors are you currently using?

Which of the disempowering behaviors do you realize you tend to use, and how has this affected your team?

What new empowering actions can you consider implementing in the future?

DEEPER DIVE

Contextual Considerations

Finally, the external context wherein empowerment is applied should be carefully considered. Typically, environments that necessitate empowerment are fast-paced and frequently changing. In such contexts, companies would have to replace slower hierarchical reporting structures with more nimble organizational designs (e.g., allowing employees at the floor or customer levels broader spans of decision-making rather than having to funnel all decisions through many layers of managerial approval).

Empowerment has been applied in many knowledge-based jobs and industries, where employees have high levels of education, training and experience, and where the focus of the work is the creation of new products, services and solutions. Research has also found that empowerment tends to occur more in service industries where presumably employees could have more leeway to adapt to their customers' needs as compared to manufacturing industries where strict procedures might need to be followed.[15] Still, even blue-collar organizations can benefit from empowering their people, provided specific conditions are set in place. A wonderful example is Morning Star, the world's largest tomato processor. With 400 blue-collar employees and a revenue of $700 million, the company practices "self-management." There are no managers and no promotions. Employees set high goals and govern themselves by mutual accountability, through peer-to-peer contracts called Colleague Letters of Understanding (CLOUs). Employees then assess each other against their CLOUs and other performance standards.

Culture is another important contextual factor. Two culture dimensions that need to be considered are power distance and uncertainty avoidance.[33]

In countries and cultures characterized as having high power distance (e.g., many Asian, Middle Eastern and Latin American cultures), there is an acceptance of the power differential between managers at the top of the hierarchy versus those at lower levels. Employees tend to defer to their managers as a sign of respect. Hence, it could be argued that empowerment might be more difficult to apply in high-power distance settings though it is not impossible as shown by the Semco Brazil example.

Interestingly, research suggests that when leaders use empowerment in high-power distance cultures, specifically Asia, employees respond more positively in terms of their task performance compared to North American settings. This could be because empowerment represents a bigger and more salient deviation from typical Asian work arrangements.[15] Clearly more research needs to be done on empowerment in different cultural settings.

Another culture dimension that could potentially affect empowerment is uncertainty avoidance. High uncertainty-avoidant cultures and countries such as Japan, Korea and Russia tend to be extremely policy and procedure-oriented in a desire to reduce ambiguity, exercise control and anticipate potential problems. Because empowerment requires a great deal of flexibility on the part of the manager, organizations in high uncertainty-avoidant cultures may need to loosen up procedures and/or specify situations in which employees can exert creativity and autonomous decision-making.

The Hofstede website provides a very useful tool to compare countries across various cultural dimensions.[34] This website can provide managers with some insight about whether and how to adapt managerial behaviors to align with different cultures.

Overall, a lot would depend on the mindset, commitment and ability of top leaders to create a strong culture of empowerment, reinforced by appropriate systems and structures. Regardless of where empowerment is applied, it is important for leaders to align their empowering approach with the context and their employees' expectations. New research suggests that if a leader's empowerment approach does not align with their employees' preferences, it may be perceived as too much or too little, thereby reducing its impact on employee engagement and performance.[17]

Takeaways

In summary, empowerment can be a powerful tool for leading, motivating and engaging employees. Here are some key takeaways from the chapter:

- Empowerment involves granting employees autonomy and authority to think, make decisions and act on their own in order to accomplish particular tasks.
- Being empowered involves being aware of the various strategies to leverage one's sources of power.
- At the core of empowerment is the leader's strong belief that each and every employee is powerful and has the potential to contribute significantly to the team and the organization.
- There are three sets of interlocking empowering leader behaviors: information sharing, participation, and feedback and support.
- Leaders must ensure that employees are ready, willing and able to be fully empowered.
- Leaders must also align empowerment strategies with the specific work context and cultural values.

Tool 7.1. Preparing for Empowerment in your Organization

Senior leaders can be skeptical about the benefits of empowering employees as an engagement strategy. The following questions can help prepare you and your colleagues in thinking through making a stronger case for empowerment as well as identifying personal and organizational changes required to support it.

a. Complete this questionnaire yourself, ask your colleagues to do the same, and discuss your answers with each other.
b. In the spirit of true empowerment, do this exercise with your employees, so you can learn more about what they expect and develop a shared understanding of empowerment within your team.

What is empowerment?

To empower means to grant authority to another individual to think, make decisions, and act on their own in order to accomplish a particular task.

1. *What would empowerment look like in our team? (Or department, organization, etc.) How would the leader and team members behave differently?*

What can we specifically do on a day-to-day basis to empower our team?

2. *What are risks related to empowerment? What are our key concerns about empowering our people? (Include managerial concerns as well as employee concerns)*

Examples could include:

- Can employees be trusted? What if they take advantage of the company?
- This is too touchy-feely. Will they still view leaders as strong and competent?
- Is there a way to balance empowerment and control?
- How can we implement this in our company, especially if it has a history of controlling management?

3. *How can leaders constructively respond to and mitigate concerns about empowerment?* What changes (personal, team, organizational) need to be put in place to support empowerment successfully within our organization?

4. *How would empowerment benefit our team and the organization as a whole?* (Benefits could include psychological outcomes, material savings or rewards, employee retention, innovation, performance improvements, etc. Include empirical evidence, such as those described in this chapter, or do additional research about best practices in your industry.)

Benefits for individual leaders and employees

Benefits for the team/department

Benefits for the organization

Suggestion: Summarize your ideas in a worksheet with 4 columns: a) Empowerment in our Team; b) Risks/Concerns; c) Leader Strategy/ Key Changes; d) Benefits.

Tool 7.2. What Sources of Power do you Frequently Use? *

Below is a list of statements that describe behaviors that leaders in work organizations can direct toward their followers. **Read each descriptive statement, thinking in terms of how often you as a leader use this to influence others.**

Use the scale to indicate the extent to which you engage in this behavior.

1=Never, 2=Sometimes, 3=Rarely, 4=Often, 5=Always.

When influencing other people in my organization...

1 2 3 4 5	1. I provide them with sound technical recommendations.
1 2 3 4 5	2. I connect them with other people who can help them.
1 2 3 4 5	3. I give them useful information to make better decisions.
1 2 3 4 5	4. I make them feel important.
1 2 3 4 5	5. I influence their compensation level.
1 2 3 4 5	6. I assign them undesirable jobs if they don't perform.

1 2 3 4 5	7. I remind them of their job commitments
1 2 3 4 5	8. I give them good job-related advice.
1 2 3 4 5	9. I help them increase their professional network.
1 2 3 4 5	10. I provide important information to help them meet their goals.
1 2 3 4 5	11. I let them know I genuinely appreciate them.
1 2 3 4 5	12. I influence their pay increases or bonuses.
1 2 3 4 5	13. I make work difficult if they don't cooperate.
1 2 3 4 5	14. I review their job requirements with them.
1 2 3 4 5	15. I share my expertise or experience.
1 2 3 4 5	16. I expose them to more people who share their interests.
1 2 3 4 5	17. I give them access to knowledge and information sources.
1 2 3 4 5	18. I make them feel personally accepted.
1 2 3 4 5	19. I influence their promotions.
1 2 3 4 5	20. I tell them I can make work unpleasant for them if they don't meet their goals.
1 2 3 4 5	21. I remind them of their job responsibilities.
1 2 3 4 5	22. I share my technical knowledge.
1 2 3 4 5	23. I introduce them to individuals they can work with or benefit from.
1 2 3 4 5	24. I provide useful information.
1 2 3 4 5	25. I make them feel important

1 2 3 4 5	26. I give them special benefits.
1 2 3 4 5	27. I tell them I can make working distasteful if they don't perform.
1 2 3 4 5	28. I emphasize their objectives and tasks.

Below is a list of the questions and the power sources associated with them. Add up your scores for each power source.

Expert power: 1, 8, 15, 22
Connection power: 2, 9, 16, 23
Information power: 3, 10, 17, 24
Referent power: 4, 11, 18, 25
Reward power: 5, 12, 19, 26
Coercive power: 6, 13, 20, 27
Legitimate power: 7, 14, 21, 28

Reflection:

- *What sources of power are you currently using the most?*
- *What sources of power might you be over-utilizing or under-utilizing?*
- *What ideas do you have to maximize, even enhance, your capacity to influence and empower others?*
- *What adjustments can you make in influencing others, and what benefits would this bring you?*

---

*Source of questionnaire: Norbom, H. M. & Lopez, P. D. (2016). Leadership and innovation: Informal power and its relationship to innovative culture. Journal of Leadership Studies, 10, 18-31.

Tool 7.3. Are you an Empowering Leader? Do's and Don'ts

Do (Empowering Behaviors)	Don't (Disempowering Behaviors)
Share information ☐ Communicate a meaningful vision and specific goals ☐ Give access to necessary information and resources ☐ Give access to internal and external customers ☐ Provide knowledge of how employee's work impacts the organization	**Hoard information** ☐ Make people feel like they are less than full members of the team or organization ☐ Leave people unclear or confused about organizational direction and where their work fits in ☐ Be a barrier to people's access to information they need to do their jobs
Encourage participation ☐ Clarify responsibilities ☐ Solicit ideas and solutions ☐ Provide autonomy in deciding how to go about tasks ☐ Gradually increase responsibilities over time as employee gains confidence	**Dominate and micromanage** ☐ Insist on making all the decisions just because you're the boss ☐ Create unnecessary approval processes to complicate or slow down the work (red tape) ☐ Frequently checking people's work as if they are incompetent

Provide constructive feedback and support	Focus on errors and weaknesses
☐ Check in regularly and give specific feedback ☐ Celebrate success, and don't punish mistakes ☐ Foster collaboration through informal activities with other employees and groups ☐ Coaching with offers of support (e.g., What do you need? How can I support your success?)	☐ Set unrealistic goals that ultimately damage people's confidence ☐ Provide feedback only when there are mistakes or areas for improvement ☐ Leave your people hanging (with no information about the progress or results of their work)

Conclusion

In this book, we introduced you to our 7-component INSPIRE model:

- **Ignite** through positive communication and meaningful work. How are you communicating positively with your team members and making their work more meaningful?

- **Nurture** your people: Are you championing the personal growth and career development of your team members?

- Leverage employee **Strengths**: How are you optimizing the strengths of your employees and your team?

- Use **Performance Management** to engage employees: Are you effectively managing the performance of your team. Are you coaching your team members on a daily basis? How do you ensure you have created a culture of accountability?

- Be **Inclusive**: What are you doing to ensure your team members feel involved, valued and fully integrated into the organization?

- **Relate** with authenticity and emotional Intelligence: Are you self-aware and cognizant of your impact on your team members? How are you creating positive relationships with your team members?

- **Empower**: Are you empowering your employees by demonstrating trust, sharing information, encouraging participation, and providing feedback and support?

Above is a diagram of our logo. There are seven birds – one for each component of the INSPIRE model. The larger bird at the top depicts the totality of successful team leadership through inspired engagement. Our key point is that all seven facets are important, and they complement each other. The size of the bird suggests the number of parts you are using – the more components you use, the higher the engagement. If you use all seven, then you will reach that largest bird, fully inspiring your team to win.

We understand that it would be overwhelming to try and apply all seven factors at once!

So here are our suggestions for future planning.

Actions:

- Which of the above components are you already doing well? From a strengths perspective, you should continue with these behaviors and try to do even better!
- You know your organization. What will work in the current culture? (However, keep an open mindset; perhaps you want to try something new.)
- Where is the low-hanging fruit, so you can capitalize on some "easy" wins?
- Perhaps one or two components really resonated with you, and you've been using some of the tools / applying some of the activities. How successful has that been? Are you seeing a difference in your relationship with your team members and/ or in their engagement?
- What were the results of the Leader's Inspire Engagement Survey? Analyze them to determine the best place on which to focus your next effort.

Common Themes

You'll note that there is some overlap among various components in this book. That is to be expected because while there are different strategies to lead, motivate and engage team members, these strategies emerge from a common leadership mindset, which views employees as being capable, competent, and motivated to perform well.

Some common themes that we have highlighted in our book are authenticity, trust and collaboration. Authenticity and trust are fundamental and deeply connected. Are you trustworthy and gen-uine? How can you demonstrate this to your team? How can you support your team to be trustworthy and authentic? Remember how the birds cooperate with each other when flying in a V formation? How can you be even more collaborative with your employees?

In various parts of the book, we have talked about the leader's role as a talent manager who seeks out team members with high levels of skill, but also diversity of perspective to allow for creativity and innovation. We have also characterized an engaging leader as one who inspires, nurtures, coaches and empowers, rather than one who tells people what to do. And finally, we have described the leader as an organizational architect who not only conveys a vision and translates this into meaningful goals, but also designs high-performance systems to ensure that these goals are translated into actionable items that are assessed and rewarded. In short, what we've tried to describe in this book is a leader with a Theory Y mindset who exhibits both the "soft" and "hard" skills to ensure team engagement as well as performance.

Sustainability

Once you've started using some of the tools, how do you sustain your behavior and the success and engagement of your team?

We recommend that you take the pulse of your team members <u>before</u> you start making changes. There are many employee engagement sur-veys you can administer. Alternatively, you could give our INSPIRE Engagement Scale (Appendix B) to your staff. This is a short survey that you can administer to your team to determine their current level of engagement. We recommend that you also administer the Team Member Assessment of Manager Behaviors Survey (Appendix C).

This gives your team members the opportunity to assess your behaviors, so you know your areas of strength and areas of opportunity. See the Appendices Introduction for instructions on their use.

To preserve anonymity and reduce bias, it's best for someone else (either from a different department, or an external consultant) to compile the results for you. Once the results are in, discuss the findings with your team, and collaboratively decide where they would like your initial focus to be. Continue with your new behaviors. Take the team pulse every six months – this will demonstrate progress you are making. Perhaps concentrate on a different component every six months.

These check-ins with your team will help you to measure your progress, identify where you should focus next, and support you in sustaining your effective behaviors. Don't forget to celebrate small wins because every little improvement builds positive feelings within yourself and your team and keeps the momentum going!

Finally, It is helpful to engage others in the process. Perhaps you could meet with other leaders in the organization to offer each other encouragement as you try out new tools / behaviors. You could also use this as a way to include and engage your team members. For example, they can develop their own leadership skills by taking the initiative in designing and implementing certain action steps and tools.

Building a motivated and engaged team involves effort and commitment from both employees and leaders. But the mutual success and feeling of pride and accomplishment, among other rewards, will be worth it.

We wish you many years of rewarding and successful leadership as you motivate your team to win at work.

Explanation of the Survey Tools (Appendices)

Appendix A: INSPIRE Engagement Behavior Survey (Leader Self-Assessment)

The Leader's Inspire Engagement Survey is a self-assessment in which you gauge your current engaging leader behaviors on a 1-5 scale. We suggest you complete this survey right away as this is your self-reported base line.

For each of the seven components, add up your score and calculate the average. Depending on how you score in each of the seven areas, you can begin reading the book starting with any of the chapters where you're strongest or the chapter that most catches your attention.

You can re-take the survey every six months. Comparisons with previous surveys will demonstrate your progress as you become an even more inspiring leader and you continue to motivate your team to win at work.

Appendix B: INSPIRE Engagement Scale (for Team Members)

The Employee Engagement Survey is a short survey that you can administer to your team members to determine their current level of engagement. (Perhaps someone in a different department could compile the results for you, so the responses are anonymous to you.) Once you have implemented some of the recommended actions in this book, you could administer it again to see the changes that have occurred. The results may also point you to the next component where you could make the most impact.

Appendix C: INSPIRE Engagement Behavior Survey (Team Member Assessment of Manager)

The Team Member Assessment Survey gives your employees the opportunity to assess your management/leadership behaviors, so you know your areas of strength and areas of opportunity.

You can compare your own rating with those of your team members.

APPENDIX A

INSPIRE Engagement Behavior Survey (Leader Self-Assessment)

Assess your engagement behaviors by completing the survey below, using the scale:

Never (N), Rarely (R), Sometimes (S), Often (O) and Always (A).

At the bottom of each section of the table, total the number of times you circle each letter. Consider your pattern:

- Which behaviors are you often or always doing? These indicate areas of strength for you.
- Which behaviors are you never or rarely doing? These suggest behaviors that you should try to do more frequently.

Ch 1: Ignite Your Team through Positive Communication and Meaningful Work

Rating	Positive Communication
N R S O A	1. I communicate an inspiring vision for the future.
N R S O A	2. I frequently discuss the importance of the work we do.
N R S O A	3. I am clear about goals and expectations.
N R S O A	4. I listen actively for understanding.
N R S O A	5. I encourage new and creative ideas.
N R S O A	6. I demonstrate appreciation for my team members' contributions.
N R S O A	7. I focus on constructive solutions to individual and team challenges.
N R S O A	8. I express confidence in my team members' abilities.

	Meaningful Work
N R S O A	1. I provide my team members with meaningful work.
N R S O A	2. I provide my team members with challenging work.

Rating	Statement
N R S O A	3. I remind my team members that their jobs are critical to the organization.
N R S O A	4. I assign my team members interesting tasks.
N R S O A	5. I provide my team members with tasks that align with their personal values.
	6. I ensure that team members are able to perform their tasks in an optimal work environment.
N R S O A	7. I encourage my team members to support one another.
N R S O A	8. I build trust within my team by being consistent in what I say and do.

Ch. 2: Nurture your people

Rating	Nurture / Employee Development
N R S O A	1. I know my team members' skills and capabilities
N R S O A	2. I know my team members' career aspirations.
N R S O A	3. I encourage my team members to take advantage of our organization's training and development opportunities.
N R S O A	4. I provide on-the-job learning opportunities to my team members.

N R S O A	5. I provide my team members with the resources necessary to support their professional development.
N R S O A	6. I have regular career development conversations with my team members.

Ch 3: Leverage Employee **Strengths** to Optimize Performance

Rating	Strengths Focus
N R S O A	1. I know my team members' strengths.
N R S O A	2. I ensure that my team members know their own strengths.
N R S O A	3. I help my team members set weekly goals based on their strengths.
N R S O A	4. I encourage my team members to learn about each other's strengths.
N R S O A	5. In one-on-one meetings, I focus the discussion on my team member's strengths.
N R S O A	6. I match job roles/responsibilities with the strengths of each team member.
N R S O A	7. I leverage my team members' strengths at work.

Ch. 4: Use **Performance Management** to Engage Employees

Rating	Performance Planning
N R S O A	1. I make sure that my team members know what is expected of them.
N R S O A	2. I discuss how each team member's work aligns with the goals of the department and the organization.
N R S O A	3. I set goals collaboratively with my team members,
N R S O A	4. I ensure that my team members have the correct tools and resources for optimal work performance.

Rating	Feedback Skills
N R S O A	1. I give frequent feedback.
N R S O A	2. I give feedback immediately.
N R S O A	3. I give specific and constructive feedback.
N R S O A	4. I recognize effective performance.
N R S O A	5. I recognize progress/improvement in performance.
N R S O A	6. I provide a system whereby team members can gauge their own progress.

Rating	Accountability
N R S O A	1. I focus on results.
N R S O A	2. I hold my team members accountable for meeting expectations and goals.
N R S O A	3. I immediately address any issues of poor performance.
N R S O A	4. I am able to deliver tough and honest feedback.
N R S O A	5. Team members know I expect them to hold each other (and myself) accountable.
N R S O A	6. I expect my team members to try and resolve conflict issues themselves before coming to me.

Ch 5: Be Inclusive

Rating	Inclusive Leadership
N R S O A	1. I am curious to learn about the interests and experiences of my team members.
N R S O A	2. I intentionally seek diverse perspectives.
N R S O A	3. I create a safe environment where team members can express themselves fully.
N R S O A	4. I build a team where team members feel a strong sense of belongingness.

N R S O A	5. I treat each team member with respect and fairness.
N R S O A	6. I ensure that my team members feel valued.
N R S O A	7. I am aware of my values and potential biases.
N R S O A	8. I build relationships across individuals and groups.
N R S O A	9. I create common goals to unite individuals and groups.

Ch. 6: **Relate** with Authenticity and Emotional Intelligence

Rating	Relate with Authenticity
N R S O A	1. I "walk my talk."
N R S O A	2. I am clear about my values and standards.
N R S O A	3. My team members know how to work with me.
N R S O A	4. I explain the rationale for important decisions.
N R S O A	5. I ask for feedback on the impact of my behavior, style and approach.

Rating	Relate with Emotional Intelligence
N R S O A	1. I can accurately describe what I'm feeling.
N R S O A	2. I know the people/situations that anger or frustrate me.
N R S O A	3. I am able to admit my own mistakes.
N R S O A	4. I have effective strategies to help me when I'm feeling angry or out of control.
N R S O A	5. I find it easy to read the emotions of others.
N R S O A	6. I recognize how my behavior affects others.
N R S O A	7. I can express my needs respectfully, even when I'm angry.
N R S O A	8. I handle conflicts skillfully.

Ch 7: Empower Your Team to Succeed

Rating	Empowering Leadership
N R S O A	1. I ensure that my team members have the requisite training to perform their jobs well.
N R S O A	2. I give my team members access to all the information they need to make key decisions at work

N R S O A	3. I give my team members the freedom to decide how to go about their work, so long as it is aligned with team and organizational objectives.
N R S O A	4. I encourage my team members to feel a strong sense of responsibility for the outcomes of their work.
N R S O A	5. I support my team members on decisions they make on the job.
N R S O A	6. I coach my team members rather than tell them what to do.

APPENDIX B

INSPIRE Engagement Scale (for Team Members)

Rate your current level of engagement at work using the following 5-point scale:

1=Strongly Disagree; 2= Disagree; 3=Neutral; 4=Agree; 5=Strongly Agree

Rating	Engagement
1 2 3 4 5	1. I am enthusiastic about going to work every day.
1 2 3 4 5	2. I feel energized at work.
1 2 3 4 5	3. I feel inspired in my job.
1 2 3 4 5	4. I take pride in the work I do.
1 2 3 4 5	5. I find it easy to immerse myself in my work.
1 2 3 4 5	6. I enjoy the work that I do.
1 2 3 4 5	7. I often give my best effort at work.

1 2 3 4 5	8. I am encouraged to contribute my knowledge and skills.
1 2 3 4 5	9. I feel like I can fully express myself at work.
1 2 3 4 5	10. I am able to use my strengths at work.
1 2 3 4 5	11. My work aligns well with my personal values.
1 2 3 4 5	12. My work gives me a sense of purpose and meaning.
1 2 3 4 5	13. I feel a strong sense of connectedness with my work colleagues.
1 2 3 4 5	14. I feel like a valued member of the organization.
1 2 3 4 5	15. I am excited about the career development opportunities at work.

- We don't yet have comparative data to confirm the classification of scores.
- However, you can examine the range and mean of the engagement scores and discuss the implications of the results with your team.

Note: This scale measures employee engagement defined as follows: "a state characterized by enthusiasm, inspiration and positive energy, psychological empowerment, and the sense of being fully connected with one's work and other people." (Hilliard & Lopez, 2019)

APPENDIX C

INSPIRE Engagement Behavior Survey (Team Member Assessment of Manager)

Consider how often your manager demonstrates the behaviors stated below. Complete the survey, using the scale:

Never (N), Rarely (R), Sometimes (S), Often (O) and Always (A).

Ch 1: Ignite through meaningful work and positive communication

Rating	Positive Communication
N R S O A	1. My manager communicates an inspiring vision for the future.
N R S O A	2. My manager discusses the importance of the work we do.
N R S O A	3. My manager is clear about goals and expectations.

N R S O A	4. My manager listens actively for understanding.
N R S O A	5. My manager encourages new and creative ideas.
N R S O A	6. My manager demonstrates appreciation for our contributions.
N R S O A	7. My manager focuses on constructive solutions to individual and team challenges.
N R S O A	8. My manager expresses confidence in our abilities.

	Meaningful Work
N R S O A	1. My manager provides us with meaningful work.
N R S O A	2. My manager provides us with challenging work.
N R S O A	3. My manager reminds us that our jobs are critical to the organization.
N R S O A	4. My manager assigns us interesting tasks.
N R S O A	5. My manager provides us with tasks that align with our personal values.
	6. My manager ensures that we are able to perform our tasks in an optimal work environment.

Rating	
N R S O A	7. My manager encourages us to support one another.
N R S O A	8. My manager builds trust within the team by being consistent in what he/she says and does.

Ch. 2: **Nurture** your people

Rating	Nurture / Employee Development
N R S O A	1. My manager knows our skills and capabilities.
N R S O A	2. My manager knows our career aspirations.
N R S O A	3. My manager encourages us to take advantage of our organization's training and development opportunities.
N R S O A	4. My manager provides us with on-the-job learning opportunities.
N R S O A	5. My manager provides us with the resources necessary to support our professional development.
N R S O A	6. My manager has regular career development conversations with us.

Ch 3: Leverage employee **Strengths**

Rating	Strengths Focus
N R S O A	1. My manager knows each of our strengths.
N R S O A	2. My manager ensures that we know the strengths of our team members.
N R S O A	3. My manager helps us set weekly goals based on our strengths.
N R S O A	4. My manager encourages us to learn about each other's strengths.
N R S O A	5. In one-on-one meetings, my manager focuses the discussion on our strengths.
N R S O A	6. My manager matches job roles/responsibilities with the strengths of each team member.
N R S O A	7. My manager leverages our strengths at work.

Ch. 4: Use **Performance Management** to engage employees

Rating	Performance Planning
N R S O A	1. My manager makes sure that we know what is expected of us.

N R S O A	2. My manager discusses how each team member's work aligns with the goals of the department and the organization.
N R S O A	3. My manager sets goals collaboratively with us.
N R S O A	4. My manager ensures that we have the correct tools and resources for optimal work performance.

Rating	Feedback Skills
N R S O A	1. My manager gives frequent feedback.
N R S O A	2. My manager gives feedback immediately.
N R S O A	3. My manager gives specific and constructive feedback.
N R S O A	4. My manager recognizes effective performance.
N R S O A	5. My manager recognizes progress/improvement in performance.
N R S O A	6. My manager provides a system whereby we can gauge our own progress.

Rating	Accountability
N R S O A	1. My manager focuses on results.
N R S O A	2. My manager holds us accountable for meeting expectations and goals.
N R S O A	3. My manager immediately addresses any issues of poor performance.
N R S O A	4. My manager is able to deliver tough and honest feedback.
N R S O A	5. We know that our manager expects us to hold each other (and him/her) accountable.
N R S O A	6. My manager expects us to try and resolve conflict issues ourselves before coming to him/her.

Ch 5: Be **Inclusive**

Rating	Inclusive Leadership
N R S O A	1. My manager is curious to learn about our interests and experiences.
N R S O A	2. My manager intentionally seeks diverse perspectives.

Rating	Item
N R S O A	3. My manager creates a safe environment where we can express ourselves fully.
N R S O A	4. My manager builds a team where we feel a strong sense of belongingness.
N R S O A	5. My manager treats each team member with respect and fairness.
N R S O A	6. My manager ensures that we feel valued.
N R S O A	7. My manager is aware of his/her values and potential biases.
N R S O A	8. My manager builds relationships across individuals and groups.
N R S O A	9. My manager creates common goals to unite individuals and groups.

Ch. 6: **Relate** with authenticity and emotional Intelligence

Rating	Authenticity
N R S O A	1. My manager "walks his/her talk."
N R S O A	2. My manager is clear about his/her values and standards.
N R S O A	3. I know how to work with my manager.
N R S O A	4. My manager explains the rationale for important decisions.

N R S O A	5. My manager asks for feedback on the impact of his/her behavior, style and approach.

Rating	Emotional Intelligence
N R S O A	1. My manager can accurately describe what he/she is feeling.
N R S O A	2. My manager knows the people/situations that anger or frustrate him/her.
N R S O A	3. My manager is able to admit his/her own mistakes.
N R S O A	4. My manager has effective strategies to help him/her when he/she is feeling angry or out of control.
N R S O A	5. My manager finds it easy to read the emotions of others.
N R S O A	6. My manager recognizes how his/her behavior affects others.
N R S O A	7. My manager can express his/her needs respectfully, even when he/she is angry.
N R S O A	8. My manager handles conflicts skillfully.

Ch 7: **Empower**

Rating	
N R S O A	1. My manager ensures that we have the requisite training to perform our jobs well.
N R S O A	2. My manager gives us access to all the information we need to make key decisions at work
N R S O A	3. My manager gives us the freedom to decide how to go about our work, so long as it is aligned with team and organizational objectives.
N R S O A	4. My manager encourages us to feel a strong sense of responsibility for the outcomes of our work.
N R S O A	5. My manager supports us on decisions we make on the job.
N R S O A	6. My manager coaches us rather than tells us what to do.

Endnotes

Preface

1. Watson, T. (2014). Why birds fly in a V formation. Retrieved from https://www.usatoday.com/story/news/nation/2014/01/15/ birds-flying-v-formation/4475687/

2. Schaufeli, W. B., Bakker, A. B., & Salanova, M. (2006). The measurement of work engagement with a short question- naire: A Cross-National Study. Educational and Psychological Measurement, 66(4), 701–716

Introduction: Leadership and the Engagement Mindset

1. Schaufeli, W. B., Salanova, M., Gonzalez-Roma, V. & Bakker, A. B. (2002). The measurement of engagement and burnout: A two-sample confirmatory-factor approach. Journal of Happiness Studies, 3(1), 71-92.

2. Kahn, W.A. (1990). Psychological conditions of personal engage- ment and disengagement at work. Academy of Management Journal, 33 (4), 692-724.

3. Hay Group (2013). Giving everyone the chance to shine: How leading organizations use engagement to drive performance

cost effectively. Retrieved from https://www.yumpu.com/en/document/read/21763569/giving-everyone-the-chance-to-shine-whitepaper-pdf-hay-group

4. Drucker Institute (2018). 2018 Drucker Institute company ranking. Retrieved from https://www.drucker.institute/2018-drucker-institute-company-ranking/.

5. Deloitte University Press (2014). Global human-capital trends 2014: Engaging the 21st century workforce. Retrieved from https://www2.deloitte.com/content/dam/insights/us/articles/hc-trends-2014-overwhelmed-employee/GlobalHumanCapitalTrends_2014.pdf

6. McGregor, D. (1960). The human side of enterprise. New York, NY: McGraw-Hill.

Chapter 1: Ignite Your Team through Positive Communication and Meaningful Work

1. Ivancevich, J. M., Konopaske, R. & Matteson, M. T. (2008). Organizational behavior and management (8th ed.). McGraw Hill/Irwin.

2. Robinson, D. & Hayday, S. (2009). The engaging manager. Institute for Employment Studies. Retrieved from https://www.employment-studies.co.uk/system/files/resources/files/470.pdf.

3. Martin, B. (2014). Manager behavior and employee engagement. Unpublished qualitative research paper. Alliant International University.

4. Carasco-Saul, M., Kim, W. & Kim, T. (2014). Leadership and employee engagement. Proposing research agendas through a review of literature. Human Resource Development Review, 14 (1), 38-63.

5. Bass, B. M. & Avolio, B. J. (1994). Transformational leadership and organizational culture. International Journal of Public Administration, 17 (3-4), 541-554.

6. Ballantyne, C. (2017). 10 most inspirational business leaders of 2017. Retrieved from https://www.huffingtonpost.com/entry/10-most-inspirational-business-leaders-of-2017_us_5a436b0fe4b0d86c803c73fc.

7. Whetten, D. A. & Cameron, K. S. (2007). Developing management skills. Pearson Prentice Hall.

8. Leibowitz, G. (2018). 13 inspiring traits of exceptional leaders. Retrieved from https://www.inc.com/glenn-leibowitz/this-is-how-exceptional-leaders-inspire-motivate-their-people.html.

9. Nancy Duarte – The secret structure of great talks. Retrieved from https://www.youtube.com/watch?v=1nYFpuc2Umk

    Simon Sinek – Start with why. How great leaders inspire action. Retrieved from https://www.youtube.com/watch?v=u4ZoJKF_VuA

    Melissa Marshall – Talk nerdy to me. Retrieved from https://www.ted.com/talks/melissa_marshall_talk_nerdy_to_me

Celeste Headlee – Ten Ways to have a better conversation. Retrieved from https://www.ted.com/talks/celeste_headlee_10_ways_to_have_a_better_conversation

10. Seo, M-G, Barrett, L. F. & Bartunek, J. M. (2004). The role of affective experience in work motivation. sAcademy of Management Review, 29 (3), 423-439.

11. Fredrickson, B. L. (2001). The role of positive emotions in positive psychology: The broaden-and-build theory of positive emotions. American Psychologist, 56 (3), 218-226.

12. Fredrickson, B. L., Conn, M. A., Coffey, K. A., Pek, J., & Finkel, S. M. (2008). Open hearts build lives: Positive emotions, induced through loving-kindness meditation, build consequential personal resources. Journal of Personality and Social Psychology, 95 (5), 1045-1062.

13. Gibb, J. (1961). Defensive communication Journal of Communication, 11 (3), 141-148.

14. Kahn, W.A. (1990). Psychological conditions of personal engagement and disengagement at work. Academy of Management Journal, 33 (4), 692-724.

15. Bibby, R. W. (2001). Canada's teens: Today, yesterday and tomorrow. Toronto, ON: Stoddart.

16. Gallup (2016). How millennials want to work and live. Retrieved from https://news.gallup.com/reports/189830/millennials-work-live.aspx.

17. Cartwright, S. & Holmes, N. (2006). The meaning of work: The challenge of regaining employee engagement and reducing cynicism. Human Resource Management Review, 16 (2), 199-208.

Hackman, J. R. & Oldham, G. R. (1976). Motivation through the design of work: Test of a theory. Organizational Behavior and Human Performance, 16 (2), 250-279.

Humphrey, S.E., Nahrgang, J.D., & Morgeson, F.P. (2007). Integrating motivational, social, and contextual work-design features: A meta-analytic summary and theoretical extension of the work-design literature. Journal of Applied Psychology, 92, 1332–1356.

18. Barrick, M.R., Mount, M. K. & Li, N. (2013). The theory of purposeful work behavior: The role of personality, higher-order goals and job characteristics. Academy of Management Review, 38 (1), 132-153.

19. Fairlie, P. (2011). Meaningful work, employee engagement and other key employee outcomes. Implications for human-resource development. Advances in Developing Human Resources, 13 (4), 508-525.

Maslow, A. (1965). Eupsychian management. Homewood, Il: Irwin.

20. Inspiringleadershipnow.com (2018). Ten of the most inspiring leaders of all time: Remarkable stories of iconic trail blazers

who went from adversity to extraordinary and redefined leadership. Retrieved from https://www.inspiringleadershipnow.com/most-inspiring-leaders-redefine-leadership/.

21. Society of Human Resource Management (2016). Employee job satisfaction and engagement. Revitalizing a changing workforce. Retrieved from https://www.shrm.org/hr-today/trends-and-forecasting/research-and-surveys/Documents/2016-Employee-Job-Satisfaction-and-Engagement-Report.pdf.

22. Stansberry, G. (n.d.). Ten examples of tremendous business leadership. Retrieved from https://www.americanexpress.com/us/small-business/openforum/articles/10-examples-of-tremendous-business-leadership-1/.

23. Huddleston, Jr., T. (2018). Uber CEO: It's time for tech founders "to take responsibility for the content of your platform." Retrieved from https://www.cnbc.com/2018/11/27/uber-ceo-khosrow-shahi-silicon-valley-needs-to-take-responsibility.html.

24. Jamrog, J. (2018). Address trust in 2018. Here are nine actions to develop it. Retrieved from https://www.i4cp.com/productivity-blog/address-trust-in-2018-here-are-nine-actions-to-develop-it.

Chapter 2: Nurture Your People

1. Deloitte (2018). 2018 Deloitte Millennial survey: Millennials disappointed in business, unprepared for industry 4.0. Retrieved from https://www2.deloitte.com/content/dam/Deloitte/global/Documents/About-Deloitte/gx-2018-millennial-survey-report.pdf.

2. Towers Watson (2014). The 2014 global workforce study: Driving engagement through a consumer-like experience. Retrieved from https://www.towerswatson.com/en-US/ Insights/IC-Types/Survey-Research-Results/2014/08/ the-2014-global-workforce-study.

3. Work Institute (2019). 2019 Retention report: Trends, reasons and a call for action. Retrieved from https://info.workinstitute.com/hubfs/2019%20Retention%20Report/Work%20 Institute%202019%20Retention%20Report%20final-1.pdf.

4. Korn Ferry (2018). Breaking boredom: Job seekers jumping ship for new challenges in 2018, according to Korn Ferry Survey. Retrieved from https://www.kornferry.com/press/ breaking-boredom-job-seekers-jumping-ship-for-new-challenges-in-2018-according-to-korn-ferry-survey

5. BlessingWhite (2017): Research report: Forget about engagement; let's talk about great days at work. Retrieved from: https://www.gpstrategies.com/wp-content/uploads/2017/09/ BlessingWhite_EngagementReportNA.pdf.

6. Gallup (2017). State of the American workplace report. Retrieved from https://www.gallup.com/workplace/238085/ state-american-workplace-report-2017.aspx.

7. Adkins, A. & Rigoni, B. (2016). Millennials want jobs to be development opportunities. Retrieved from https://www.gallup.com/workplace/236438/millennials-jobs-development-opportunities.aspx.

8. Lierz, K. (2018). How T-Mobile reinvented its career development

programs. Retrieved from https://www.i4cp.com/interviews/how-t-mobile-reinvented-its-career-development-programs.

9. BlessingWhite (2014, p. 8). Navigating ambiguity: Career research 2014. Career plans are worthless, but planning is everything. Retrieved from https://blessingwhite.com/navigating-ambiguity-career-research-report-2014/.

10. Gallup (2016). How Millennials want to work and live. Retrieved from https://www.gallup.com/workplace/238073/millennials-work-live.aspx.

11. Giannosa, J. (2017). Career ladders vs. career lattices – Tools for employee development. Retrieved from https://www.edsisolutions.com/blog/career-ladders-vs-career-lattices-tools-for-employee-development.

12. Goldberg, E. L & Associates. (N.D.). Engaging and retaining talent through better career management. Retrieved from http://www.elgoldberg.com/case-studies-engaging-and-retaining-talent.

13. Finkelstein, S. (2019). Why a one-size-fits-all approach to employee development doesn't work. Retrieved from https://hbr.org/2019/03/why-a-one-size-fits-all-approach-to-employee-development-doesnt-work.

14. BlessingWhite (2018). The managers role in career development. Retrieved from https://blessingwhite.com/the-managers-role-in-career-development/.

15. Faison Roe, D. J. (2019). When a top performer wants to leave, should you try to stop them? Retrieved from https://

hbr.org/2019/03/when-a-top-performer-wants-to-leave-should-you-try-to-stop-them?utm_medium=email&utm_source=newsletter_daily&utm_campaign=dailyalert_active-subs&utm_content=signinnudge&referral=00563&deliveryName=DM31874.

Chapter 3: Leverage Employee Strengths to Optimize Performance

1. Buckingham, M., & Clifton, D. O. (2001). Now, discover your strengths. New York, NY: The Free Press.

2. Linley, A. (2008, p. 9). Average to A+: Realising strengths in yourself and others. Coventry, UK: CAPP Press.

3. Medland, D. (2013). Lord Davies: How he leapt outside his comfort zone. Retrieved from https://www.ft.com/content/36d8d182-2786-11e3-8feb-00144feab7de.

4. Farrell, S. (2009). Mervyn Davies profile: A man trusted by City and the PM. Retrieved from https://www.independent.co.uk/news/business/news/mervyn-davies-profile-a-man-trusted-by-city-and-the-pm-1366863.html.

5. Meiling, T. (2018). Most of your managers are only doing 50% of their jobs. Retrieved from https://strengthsschool.com/strengthsfinder-blog/most-of-your-managers-are-only-doing-50-of-their-jobs.

6. Csikszentmihalyi, M. (1997). Finding flow: The psychology of engagement with everyday life. New York, NY: Basic Books.

7. Rath, T. & Conchie, B. (2008). Strengths based leadership. New York, NY: Gallup, Inc.

8. Peterson, C. & Seligman, M. E. P. (2004). Character strengths and virtues: A handbook and classification. Washington, DC: American Psychological Association.

9. Corporate Leadership Council. (2002) Building the high-performance workforce. Washington, D.C.: Corporate Executive Board.

10. Gallup (2017). State of the American workplace report. Retrieved from https://www.gallup.com/workplace/238085/state-american-workplace-report-2017.aspx.

11. Quantum (2018). 2018 Employee engagement trends among America's best places to work. Retrieved from https://www.quantumworkplace.com/2018-employee-engagement-trends-report.

SHRM (2016). 2016 Employee job satisfaction and engagement: Revitalizing a changing workforce. A research report. Retrieved from https://www.shrm.org/hr-today/trends-and-forecasting/research-and-surveys/Pages/Job-Satisfaction-and-Engagement-Report-Revitalizing-Changing-Workforce.aspx.

The Strengths Lab (2019). The strengths lab 2019 workplace survey: The impact of putting our strengths to work. Retrieved from https://www.michellemcquaid.com/5-ways-help-workers-develop-strengths/?utm_source=Ontraport&utm_medium=email&utm_content=20190426-Missing-Strengths-Development-3&utm_campaign=MMQ001

12. Harter, J., & Adkins, A. (2015). Employees want a lot more from their managers. Retrieved from http://www.gallup.com/businessjournal/182321/employees-lot-managers.aspx.

13. Gallup (2016). How millennials want to work and live. Retrieved from https://www.gallup.com/workplace/238073/millennials-work-live.aspx.

14. Linley, A. (2018). Can you turn your weaknesses into a strength? Retrieved from https://www.michellemcquaid.com/can-turn-weaknesses-strength/.

15. Buffett, W. (2007). Buffett's words at a meeting. Retrieved from https://buffett.cnbc.com/video/2007/05/05/morning-session---2007-berkshire-hathaway-annual-meeting.html?&start=8467&end=8755.

16. Buckingham, M. (2007). Go put your strengths to work: 6 powerful steps to achieve outstanding performance. New York, NY: Free Press.

    Loomis, C. J. (2006). A conversation with Warren Buffett. Retrieved from https://money.cnn.com/2006/06/25/magazines/fortune/charity2.fortune/index.htm.

17. Clifton, D. O. & Harter, J. K. (2003). Investing in Strengths. In A.K.S. Cameron, B. J. E. Dutton & C. R. E. Quinn (Eds.), Positive organizational scholarship: Foundations of a new discipline (pp. 111-121). San Francisco: Berrett-Koehler Publishers, Inc.

    Isogo, 2018. What is the strengths perspective? Speed reading study explained better than ever. Retrieved from https://www.isogostrong.com/strengthsfinder-speed-reading/.

18. Gallup (2013). State of the American workplace. Employee engagement insights for U.S. business leaders. Retrieved from gallup.com.

19. Asplund, J., Harter, J. K., Agrawal, S., & Plowman, S. (2016). The relationship between strengths-based employee development and organizational outcomes: 2015 Strengths meta-analysis. Retrieved from Gallup.com.

20. Asplund, J. & Blacksmith, N. (2011). Making strengths-based development work: Effective implementation and support are vital to a program's success. Retrieved from http://businessjournal.gallup.com/content/148691/Making-Strengths-Based-Development-Work.aspx.

Sorenson, S. (2014). How employees' strengths make your company stronger. Retrieved from https://news.gallup.com/businessjournal/167462/employees-strengths-company-stronger.aspx.

21. Asplund, J. & Blacksmith, N. (2011). How strengths boost engagement. Retrieved from https://news.gallup.com/businessjournal/146972/Strengths-Boost-Engagement.aspx.

22. Roche, B. & Hefferon, K. (2013). The assessment needs to go hand-in hand with the debriefing: The importance of a structured coaching debriefing in understanding and applying a positive psychology strengths assessment. International Coaching Psychology Review, Vol 8 No. 1, 20-34.

23. McQuaid, M. (2015). The 2015 Strengths at Work survey - VIA Institute on character. Retrieved from https://www.

michellemcquaid.com/product/2015-strengths-at-work-survey/.

24. Biswas-Diener, R., Kashdan, T, B. and Minhas, G. (2011). A dynamic approach to psychological strength development and intervention. The Journal of Positive Psychology, 6: 2, 106 — 118.

25. Linley, A. (2008, p. 58). Average to A+: Realising strengths in yourself and others. Coventry, UK: CAPP Press.

26. Buckingham, M. & Goodall, A. (2019). The power of hidden teams: The most-engaged employees work together in ways companies don't even realize. Retrieved from https://hbr.org/cover-story/2019/05/the-power-of-hidden-teams

27. Sorenson, S. (2014). How employees' strengths make your company stronger. Retrieved from https://news.gallup.com/businessjournal/167462/employees-strengths-company-stronger.aspx.

28. Fernandez and Houle (2015). An effective strengths program: Cardinal Health case study. Retrieved from https://www.gallup.com/workplace/236588/effective-strengths-program-cardinal-health-case-study.aspx.

29. Gallup (2015). Case study: Creating cultural transformation with a strengths-based approach. Retrieved from gallup.com.

O'Bannon, B. (2018). Let's talk strengths: Applying your strengths to grow stronger, work smarter, and live richer. Sherman, TX: Strengths Champion Publishing.

Chapter 4: Use Performance Management to Engage Employees

1. BlessingWhite (2013). Employee engagement research update. Beyond the numbers: A practical approach for individuals, managers, and executives. Retrieved from https://blessingwhite. com/employee-engagement-research-report-update-jan-2013/.

    Mone, E., Eisinger, C., Guggenheim, K., Price, B., & Stine, C. (2011) Performance management at the wheel: Driving employee engagement in organizations. Journal of Business Psychology, 26:205-212.

    Mone, E., & London, M. (2010). Employee engagement through effective performance management: A practical guide for managers. New York: Routledge.

2. Gallup (2015). State of the American manager: Analytics and advice for leaders. Retrieved from https://www.gallup.com/ser-vices/182138/state-american-manager.aspx.

3. BlessingWhite (2017). Research Report: Forget about engagement; let's talk about great days at work. Retrieved from https://www.gpstrategies.com/wp-content/uploads/2017/09/ BlessingWhite_EngagementReportNA.pdf.

    BlessingWhite (2013). Employee engagement research update. Beyond the numbers: A practical approach for individuals, managers, and executives. Retrieved from https://blessingwhite. com/employee-engagement-research-report-update-jan-2013/.

4. Mone, E., & London, M. (2010). Employee engagement through effective performance management: A practical guide for managers. New York: Routledge.

5. Connors, R, & Smith, T. (2015). Cracking the employee engagement code. Retrieved from https://trainingmag.com/ cracking-employee-engagement-code.

6. Wigert, B. & Harter, J. (2017). Re-engineering performance management. Retrieved from https://www.gallup.com/work-place/238064/re-engineering-performance-management.aspx.

7. BlessingWhite (2013). Employee engagement research update. Beyond the numbers: A practical approach for individuals, managers, and executives. Retrieved from https://blessingwhite.com/employee-engagement-research-report-update-jan-2013/.

8. Robinson, D., & Hayday, S. (2009). The engaging manager. Report 470, Institute for Employment Studies. Retrieved from https://www.employment-studies.co.uk/system/files/resources/ files/470.pdf.

9. BlessingWhite (2017). Research Report: Forget about engagement; let's talk about great days at work. Retrieved from https://www.gpstrategies.com/wp-content/uploads/2017/09/ BlessingWhite_EngagementReportNA.pdf.

Mone, E., & London, M. (2010). Employee engagement through effective performance management: A practical guide for managers. New York: Routledge.

10. 2013 Society for Human Resource Management in Finkelstein, S. (2015). What amazing bosses do differently. Retrieved from https://hbr.org/2015/11/what-amazing-bosses-do-differently.

11. Gallup (2016). How Millennials want to work and live. Retrieved from https://www.gallup.com/workplace/238073/millennials-work-live.aspx.

12. Sylvester, D. (2018). How Booz Allen created an inclusive culture of performance feedback. Retrieved from https://www.i4cp.com/interviews/how-booz-allen-created-an-inclusive-culture-of-performance-feedback.

13. Buckingham, M., & Goodall, A. (2019). The feedback fallacy. Retrieved from https://hbr.org/2019/03/the-feedback-fallacy.

    Jack, A. I., Boyatzis, R. E., Khawaja, M. S., Passarelli, A. M. & Leckie, R. L. (2013). Visioning in the brain: An fMRI study of inspirational coaching and mentoring. Social Neuroscience, 8:4, 369-384.

14. BlessingWhite (2016). Research report: The coaching conundrum – Coaching in the post-performance-assessment era. Retrieved from https://blessingwhite.com/the-coaching-conundrum-report-2016/.

15. Garvin, D.A. (2013). How Google sold its engineers on management. Retrieved from https://hbr.org/2013/12/how-google-sold-its-engineers-on-management.

16. Tarallo, M. (2018). The art of servant leadership. Retrieved from https://www.shrm.org/ResourcesAndTools/hr-topics/

organizational-and-employee-development/Pages/The-Art-of-Servant-Leadership.aspx.

17. Whitmore, J. (2017). Coaching for performance Fifth Edition: The principles and practice of coaching and leadership. Updated 25th Anniversary Edition. London: Nicholas Brealey. Publishing.

18. Connors, R., Smith, T. & Hickman, C. (2004). The Oz Principle. New York, NY: The Penguin Group.

19. Custom Insight (2013). What drives the most engaged employees? Retrieved from http://www.custominsight.com/ employee-engagement-survey/research-employee-engagement. asp.

20. Grenny, J. (2014). The best teams hold themselves accountable. Retrieved from https://hbr.org/2014/05/ the-best-teams-hold-themselves-accountable.

21. Corporate Leadership Council (2002). Building the high-performance workforce: A quantitative analysis of the effectiveness of performance management strategies. Corporate Executive Board.

22. Willis Towers Watson (2016). Performance management isn't working: Programs not keeping up with evolving business needs. Retrieved from https://www.towerswatson.com/ en-US/Insights/IC-Types/Survey-Research-Results/2015/12/ performance-management-isnt-working-programs-not-keeping-up-with-evolving-business-needs.

23. Sutton, R. & Wigert, B. (2019). More harm than good: The truth about performance reviews. Retrieved from https://tinyurl.com/yxqdh9pf

24. Bakalar, K (2015). 5 Ways to make good managers great coaches. Retrieved from http://blessingwhite.com/article/2015/10/22/5-ways-to-make-good-managers-great-coaches/.

25. Finkelstein, S. (2015a). The dreaded performance review. Retrieved from http://www.bbc.com/capital/story/20150826-the-dreaded-performance-review.

26. Adobe, 2019. How Adobe retired performance reviews and inspired great performance. Retrieved from https://www.adobe.com/check-in.html.

Doerr, J. (2018). How did Adobe stop its best employees from leaving? It killed annual performance reviews. You could do the same. Retrieved from https://www.linkedin.com/pulse/how-did-adobe-stop-its-best-employees-from-leaving-killed-john-doerr/.

Chapter 5: Be Inclusive

1. Downey, S. N., van der Werff, L., Thomas, K. M., & Plaut, V. C. (2015). Diversity practices and engagement. Journal of Applied Social Psychology, 45, 35-44.

Mor Barak, M. E. (2005). Managing diversity: Toward a globally inclusive workplace. Thousand Oaks, CA: Sage.

2.   Myers, V. (2012). Diversity is being asked to the party. Inclusion is being asked to dance. GPSolo E-report, 1(11). Retrieved from www.americanbar.org/groups/gpsolo/publications/gpsolo_ereport/2012/june_2012/diversity_invited_party_inclusion_asked_dance.html.

3.   Garr, S. S. (2014). The diversity and inclusion benchmarking report: An analysis of the current landscape. Bersin by Deloitte.

4.   PwC (2017). Global diversity and inclusion survey. Retrieved from https://www.pwc.com/gx/en/services/people-organisation/global-diversity-and-inclusion-survey.html.

5.   Turner, C. (2012). Difference works: Improving retention, productivity and profitability through inclusion. Live Oak Book Company.

6.   Milam, J. (2012). Why workplace friendships matter: An assessment of workplace friendships, employee engagement, job embeddedness, and job burnout. Alliant International University. Doctoral dissertation.

7.   Downey, S. N., van der Werff, L., Thomas, K. M., & Plaut, V. C. (2015). Diversity practices and engagement. Journal of Applied Social Psychology, 45, 35-44.

8.   Maslow, A. H. (1943). Preface to motivation theory. Psychosomatic Medicine, 5, 85-92.

9.   Shellenbarger, S. (2018). Why perks no longer cut it for workers. Retrieved from https://www.wsj.com/articles/why-perks-no-longer-cut-it-for-workers-1543846157.

10. Ryan, R. M. & Deci, E. L. (2000). Self-determination theory and the facilitation of intrinsic motivation, social development and well-being. American Psychologist, 55 (1), 68-78.

11. Kahn, W.A. (1990). Psychological conditions of personal engagement and disengagement at work. Academy of Management Journal, 33 (4), 692-724.

12. Ferdman, B. M. (2014). The Practice of inclusion in diverse organizations. In Diversity at work: The practice of inclusion (Eds B. M. Ferdman and B. R. Deane). John Wiley & Sons.

13. Robinson, D., Perryman, S. & Hayday, S. (2004). The drivers of employee engagement. Institute of Employment Studies. Retrieved from www.employment-studies.co.uk/system/files/resources/files/408.pdf.

14. Cottrill, K., Lopez, P.D., & Hoffman, C. C. (2014). How authentic leadership and inclusion benefit organizations. Equality, Diversity and Inclusion: An International Journal, 33 (3), 275-292.

15. PwC (2014). Engaging and empowering Millennials. A follow-up to PwC's NextGen global generational study. Retrieved from https://www.pwc.com/gx/en/hr-management-services/publications/assets/pwc-engaging-and-empowering-millennials.pdf.

16. Abadi, M. (2018). The job market is so hot right now that workers are "ghosting" employers without even saying goodbye. Retrieved from https://www.businessinsider.com/workers-ghosting-jobs-quitting2018-12.

17. Shapiro, G., Wells, H. & Saunders, R. (2011). Inclusive lead-
     ership: From pioneer to mainstream. Maximising the potential
     of your people. Opportunity Now in partnership with Shapiro
     Consulting. Retrieved from gender.bitc.org.uk/system/files/
     research/inclusive_leadership_-_from_pioneer_to_main-
     stream.pdf.

18. Randel, A. E., Dean, M. A., Ehrhart, K. H., Chung, B., &
     Shore, L. (2016). Leader inclusiveness, psychological diver-
     sity climate, and helping behaviors. Journal of Managerial
     Psychology, 31 (1), 216-234.

19. Prime, J. & Salib, E. R. (2014). Inclusive leadership: The view
     from six countries. New York, NY: Catalyst.

20. Duhigg, C. (2016). What Google learned from its quest
     to build the perfect team. Retrieved from www.nytimes.
     com/2016/02/28/magazine/what-google-learned-from-its-
     quest-to-build-the-perfect-team.html?_r=0.

21. Bersin, J. (2019). Why diversity and inclusion has become a busi-
     ness priority. Retrieved from https://joshbersin.com/2015/12/
     why-diversity-and-inclusion-will-be-a-top-priority-for-2016/

22. Bourke, 2016, as cited in Bourke, J. & Dillon, B. (2019).
     The diversity and inclusion revolution: Eight powerful truths.
     Deloitte Review, 22. Retrieved from https://www2.deloitte.
     com/insights/us/en/deloitte-review/issue-22/diversity-and-in-
     clusion-at-work-eight-powerful-truths.html.

23. Hunt, V., Yee, L., Prince, S. & Dixon-Fyle, S. (2018). Delivering
     through diversity. McKinsey & Company. Retrieved from

https://www.mckinsey.com/business-functions/organization/our-insights/delivering-through-diversity.

24. PR Newswire (2018). Sodexho recognized as a top company for diversity by Diversity Inc. for 10 consecutive years. Retrieved from https://www.prnewswire.com/news-releases/sodexo-recognized-as-a-top-company-for-diversity-by-diversityinc-for-10-consecutive-years-300641999.html.

25. Leanin.org & McKinsey & Company (2018). Women in the workplace 2018. Retrieved from https://www.mckinsey.com/business-functions/organization/our-insights/delivering-through-diversity.

Sodexho (2019). Pressing for gender balance. Retrieved from https://www.sodexo.com/gender-balance.html.

26. Thomson Reuters (2018). Thomson Reuters D&I index ranks the 2018 top 100 most diverse and inclusive organizations globally. Retrieved from https://www.thomsonreuters.com/en/press-releases/2018/september/thomson-reuters-di-index-ranks-the-2018-top-100-most-diverse-and-inclusive-organizations-globally.html.

27. Accenture (2018). Accenture ranks no. 1 on Thomson Reuters Index of world's most diverse and inclusive companies. Retrieved from https://newsroom.accenture.com/news/accenture-ranks-no-1-on-thomson-reuters-index-of-worlds-most-diverse-and-inclusive-companies.htm.

28. Dantes, D. (2019). Accenture CEO: Diversity and inclusion start from within. Retrieved from http://fortune.

com/2019/01/08/accenture-ceo-julie-sweet-ceo-initiative/.

29. Forbes (2019). The best employers for diversity 2019. Retrieved from https://www.forbes.com/lists/best-employers-diversity/#3af349916468.

Richards, S. & Munster, D. (2018). Bold and inclusive leadership: The time is now. Retrieved from https://www.diversitybestpractices.com/sites/diversitybestpractices.com/files/attachments/2018/11/5af4dde6-eae8-410c-92a7-19f7e2cd89642f6946903280_insight_paper-bold_and_inclusive_leadership_5.pdf.

U.S. Bank, (2016). 2016 Corporate responsibility report. Retrieved from https://www.usbank.com/en/corporate_responsibility/diversity-and-inclusion.html.

30. Bourke, J. and Dillon, B. Dillon (2016). The six signature traits of inclusive leadership: Thriving in a diverse new world. Deloitte University Press.

EU Project on Inclusive Leadership (2018). Inclusive Leadership. Retrieved from https://inclusiveleadership.eu/about/project/.

Prime, J. & Salib, E. R. (2014). Inclusive leadership: The view from six countries.   New York, NY: Catalyst.

Richards, S. & Munster, D. (2018). Bold and inclusive leadership: The time is now. Retrieved from https://www.diversitybestpractices.com/sites/diversitybestpractices.com/files/attachments/2018/11/5af4dde6-eae8-410c-92a7-

19f7e2cd89642f6946903280_insight_paper-bold_and_inclusive_leadership_5.pdf.

31. Avolio, B. J., Gardner, W. L., Walumbwa, F. O., Luthans, F., & May, D. R. (2004). Unlocking the mask: A look at the process by which authentic leaders impact follower attitudes and behaviors. The Leadership Quarterly, 15 (6), 801-823.

32. Linley, A. (2008). Average to A+: Realising strengths in yourself and others (Strengthening the world). CAPP Press.

33. Bourke, J. and Dillon, B. Dillon (2016). The six signature traits of inclusive leadership: Thriving in a diverse new world. Deloitte University Press.

34. Leanin.org & McKinsey & Company (2018). Women in the workplace 2018. Retrieved from https://www.mckinsey.com/business-functions/organization/our-insights/delivering-through-diversity.

35. Moran, G. (2017). How these top companies are getting inclusion right. Retrieved from https://www.fastcompany.com/3067346/how-these-top-companies-are-getting-inclusion-right.

36. Mozilla (2018). Mozilla community participation guidelines. Retrieved from https://www.mozilla.org/en-US/about/governance/policies/participation/.

37. Finkelstein, S. (2017). 4 ways managers can be more inclusive. Retrieved from https://hbr.org/2017/07/4-ways-managers-can-be-more-inclusive.

38. Chugh, D. (2018). How PwC's Tim Ryan learned to talk about race (and you can, too). Retrieved from https://www.forbes.com/sites/dollychugh/2018/12/06/how-pwcs-tim-ryan-learned-to-talk-about-race-and-how-you-can-too/#4b505c8738a2.

Perna, G. (2019). Why PwC's chairman Tim Ryan's top priority is diversity and race. Retrieved from https://chiefexecutive.net/pwc-chairman-tim-ryan-top-priority-diversity-race/.

39. CEO action for diversity and inclusion (N.D.). Retrieved from www.ceoaction.com

40. David, S. (2014). Inclusiveness means giving every employee personal attention. Retrieved from https://hbr.org/2014/06/inclusiveness-means-giving-every-employee-personal-attention.

41. Allport, G. W. (1954). The nature of prejudice. Cambridge, MA: Addison-Wesley.

42. Ensari, N. K., & Miller, N. (2006). The Application of the Personalization Model in diversity management. Group Processes & Intergroup Relations, 9(4), 589–607.

Chapter 6: Relate with Authenticity and Emotional Intelligence

1. BlessingWhite (2017): Research report: Forget about engagement; let's talk about great days at work. Retrieved from: https://www.gpstrategies.com/wp-content/uploads/2017/09/BlessingWhite_EngagementReportNA.pdf

Crim, D,. & Seijts, G. (2006) What engages employees the most or, the ten C's of employee engagement. Retrieved from: http://www.iveybusinessjournal.com/topics/the-workplace/ what-engages-employees-the-most-or-the-ten-cs-of-employee-engagement

2.   SHRM (2012). Foundation Executive Briefing. Employee engagement: Your competitive advantage. Retrieved from https://www.shrm.org/ResourcesAndTools/business-solutions/ Documents/Engagement%20Briefing-FINAL.pdf.

3.   3 BlessingWhite (2018). 2018 Research report. Tomorrow's leaders today: What leaders need right now, and in the future, to be successful. Retrieved from https://blessingwhite.com/ tomorrows-leaders-today-what-leaders-say-they-need-right-now-and-in-the-future-to-be-successful/.

DDI, The Conference Board & EY. (2018). Global leadership forecast 2018: 25 research insights to fuel your people strategy. Retrieved from https://www.ey.com/Publication/vwLUAssets/ ey-the-global-leadership-forecast/$FILE/ey-the-global-leader-ship-forecast.pdf.

4.   Gallup (2018). Gallup's perspective on: Designing your organization's employee experience. Retrieved from https://www.gallup.com/access/239222/employee-experience-surveys.aspx.

5.   Harter, J. & Adkins, A. (2015). Employees want a lot more from their managers. Retrieved from http://www.gallup.com/ businessjournal/182321/employees-lot-managers.aspx.

6.   Armstrong, A., Olivier, S, & Wilkinson, S (2018). Shades

of grey: An exploratory study of engagement in work teams. Retrieved from: http://hultmedia.ef-cdn.com/~/media/hult-edu/executive-education/research/shades%20of%20grey. pdf?la=en.

7.   Great Place to Work (2017). Report: The executive's guide to engaging Millennials. Retrieved from   http://www.6seconds.org/2014/01/02/employee-engagement-emotional-intelligence/.

8.   Gallup (2016). How Millennials want to work and live. Retrieved from https://www.gallup.com/workplace/238073/millennials-work-live.aspx.

9.   BlessingWhite (2018). 2018 Research report. Tomorrow's leaders today: What leaders need right now, and in the future, to be successful. Retrieved from https://blessingwhite.com/tomorrows-leaders-today-what-leaders-say-they-need-right-now-and-in-the-future-to-be-successful/.

10.   Armstrong, A., Olivier, S, & Wilkinson, S (2018). Shades of grey: An exploratory study of engagement in work teams. Retrieved from: http://hultmedia.ef-cdn.com/~/media/hult-edu/executive-education/research/shades%20of%20grey. pdf?la=en.

Vogelgesang, G. R., Leroy, H., & Avolio, B. J. (2013). The mediating effects of leader integrity with transparency in communication and work engagement/performance. The Leadership Quarterly, 24(3), 405-413.

11.   Rice, C. (2007). Driving long-term engagement through a

high-performance culture. In Finney, M.I. Building high-performance people and organizations, Vol 2. The engaged workplace: Organizational strategies, pp 30-47. Praeger: Westport, Connecticut.

12. Penger, S., & Černe, M. (2014) Authentic leadership, employees' job satisfaction, and work engagement: A hierarchical linear modelling approach, Economic Research-Ekonomska Istraživanja, 27:1, 508-526.

13. Gallup (2015). State of the American manager: Analytics and advice for leaders. Retrieved from https://www.gallup.com/services/182138/state-american-manager.aspx.

14. Armstrong, A., Olivier, S, & Wilkinson, S (2018). Shades of grey: An exploratory study of engagement in work teams. Retrieved from: http://hultmedia.ef-cdn.com/~/media/hult-edu/executive-education/research/shades%20of%20grey.pdf?la=en.

15. George, B. (2015). The true qualities of authentic leaders. Retrieved from https://www.forbes.com/sites/hbsworkingknowledge/2015/11/10/the-true-qualities-of-authentic-leaders/#7a2e13b6f74d.

George, B. (2013). Authentic leadership: Rediscovering the secrets to creating lasting value. San Francisco, CA: Jossey-Bass

Knowledge at Wharton (2014). Bill George: Authentic leadership and letting your strengths "bloom." Retrieved from http://knowledge.wharton.upenn.edu/article/authentic-leadership/.

16. Genos International (2015). Leadership emotional intelligence and employee engagement – IBM. Retrieved from https://www.genosinternational.com/ibm-case-study/.

17. Goleman, D., Boyatzis, R., & McKee, A. (2002). Primal leadership: Realizing the power of emotional intelligence. Boston, MA: Harvard Business School Press.

18. Gentry, W.A, Weber, T.J., & Sadri, G. (2007). Empathy in the workplace: A tool for effective leadership. White paper, Center for Creative Leadership. Retrieved from https://www.ccl.org/wp-content/uploads/2015/04/EmpathyInTheWorkplace.pdf.

19. Gallup (2016). How millennials want to work and live. Retrieved from https://www.gallup.com/workplace/238073/millennials-work-live.aspx.

Chapter 7: Empower Your Team to Succeed

1. Hewko, J. (2018). This is what Millennials want. Retrieved from https://www.weforum.org/agenda/2018/01/this-is-what-millennials-want-in-2018/.

2. Cenkus,B. (2017). Millennials aren't entitled. They are empowered. Retrieved from https://qz.com/work/1143591/millennials-arent-entitled-they-are-empowered/.

3. Workplace Trends (2015). The Millennial leadership survey. Retrieved from https://workplacetrends.com/the-millennial-leadership-survey/.

4. Choi, J. (2006). A motivational theory of charismatic

leadership: Envisioning, empathy and empowerment. Journal of Leadership and Organizational Studies, 13 (1), 24-43.

Spreitzer, G. M. (1995). Psychological empowerment in the workplace: Construct definition, measurement, and validation. Academy of Management Journal, 23, 601-629.

5. Carbonara, S. (2013). Manager's guide to employee engagement. McGraw-Hill.

6. McGregor, D. (1960). The human side of enterprise. New York: McGraw-Hill.

7. Randolph, W. M. & Kemery, E. R. (2010). Managerial uses of power basis in a model of managerial empowerment practices and employee psychological empowerment. Journal of Leadership and Organizational Studies, 18 (1), 95-106.

8. Sweeney, C. & Gosfield, J. (2014). No managers required: How Zappos ditched the old corporate structure for something new. Retrieved from https://www.fastcompany.com/3024358/no-managers-required-how-zappos-ditched-the-old-corporate-structure-for-somethin.

9. Zapposinsights.com (n.d.) Holacracy and self-organization. Retrieved from https://www.zapposinsights.com/about/holacracy.

10. Fortune Magazine (2015). 100 best companies to work for, 2015. Retrieved from http://fortune.com/best-companies/2015/zappos-com-86/.

Hughes, F. (2018). Zappos CEO shows exactly why "doing good is good business." Retrieved from https://www.digitalistmag.com/future-of-work/2018/06/13/zappos-ceo-shows-exactly-why-doing-good-is-good-business-06175847.

11. Spreitzer G. M. (1992). When organizations dare: The dynamics of individual empowerment in the workplace. Unpublished doctoral dissertation. University of Michigan.

    Whetten, D. A. & Cameron, K. S. (2007). Developing management skills. Pearson Prentice Hall.

12. Kahn, W.A. (1990). Psychological conditions of personal engagement and disengagement at work. Academy of Management Journal, 33 (4), 692-724.

13. Ryan, R. M. & Deci, E. L. (2000). Self-determination theory and the facilitation of intrinsic motivation, social development and well-being. American Psychologist, 55 (1), 68-78.

14. Garvin, D. (2013, Dec.). How Google sold its engineers on management. Retrieved from https://hbr.org/2013/12/how-google-sold-its-engineers-on-management.

15. Yang, S. & Choi, S. O. (2009). Employee empowerment and team performance: autonomy, responsibility, information and creativity. Team Performance Management: An International Journal, 15 (5/6), 289-301.

16. Seibert, S. E., Wang, G. & Courtright, S. H. (2011). Antecedents and consequences of psychological and team empowerment in organizations: A meta-analytic Review. Journal of Applied

Psychology, 96(5), 981-1003.

17. Kirkman, B. L. & Rosen, B. (2017). Beyond self-management. Antecedents and consequences of team empowerment. Academy of Management Journal, 42 (1).

18. Lee, A, Willis, S, Tian, AW (2018). Empowering leadership: A meta‑analytic examination of incremental contribution, mediation, and moderation. Journal of Organizational Behavior. 39,306–325.

19. Raven, B. H. (2008). The bases of power and the power/interaction model of interpersonal influence. Analyses of Social Issues and Public Policy, 8 (1), 1-22.

20. Norbom, H. M. & Lopez, P. D. (2016). Leadership and innovation: Informal power and its relationship to innovative culture. Journal of Leadership Studies, 10, 18-31.

21. Whetten, D. A. & Cameron, K. S. (2007). Developing management skills. Pearson Prentice Hall.

22. Denning, S. (2012). A glimpse at a workplace of the future: Valve. Retrieved from www.forbes.com/sites/stevedenning/2012/04/27/a-glimpse-at-a-workplace-of-the-future-valve/#275a06177557.

     Kellion, L. (2013). Valve: How going boss-free empowered the games-maker. Retrieved from www.bbc.com/news/technology-24205497.

23. Perkins, A. (2017). Do results-only workplaces really

work? Retrieved from www.business.com/articles/do-results-only-workplaces-really-work/.

Perkins, A. (2014). Do results-only work environments really work? Retrieved from http://outsideincompanies.com/do-results-only-work-environments-really-work/.

24. Kohl, A. (2018). What employees really want at work. Retrieved from https://www.forbes.com/sites/alankohll/2018/07/10/what-employees-really-   want-at-work/#469eaf9d5ad3.

25. Allen, T. D. (2013). The work–family role Interface: A synthesis of the research from industrial and organizational Psychology. In N. W. Schmitt & S. Highhouse (Eds.), Handbook of psychology Vol. 12, Industrial and organizational psychology, 2nd ed. (pp. 698-718). Hoboken, NJ: John Wiley & Sons.

Noonan, M. C., & Glass, J. L. (2012). The hard truth about telecommuting. Monthly Labor Review, 135(6), 38-45. Retrieved from https://www.bls.gov/opub/mlr/2012/06/art-3full.pdf.

26. Chung, H. (2018). Gender, flexibility stigma and the perceived negative consequences of flexible working in the UK. Social Indicators Research, 1-25.

27. Abdi, N. (2017). 4 examples of how companies effectively engage their employees. Retrieved from https://blog.talaera.com/2017/07/19/companies-empower-engage-employees.

28. Adobe (2017). The hovering art director. Retrieved from https://www.youtube.com/watch?v=1C75bKax4Eg

29. Semler, R. (1994). Why my former employees still work for me. Retrieved from https://hbr.org/1994/01/why-my-former-employees-still-work-for-me.

   Semler, R. (1989). Managing without managers. Retrieved from https://hbr.org/1989/09/managing-without-managers.

30. Semco Partners (n.d.). Joint-venture catalysts for expansion in Brazil. Retrieved from http://www.semco.com.br/en/.

31. Maddux, W.W. & Swaab, I.R. (2014). Ricardo Semler: A revolutionary model of leadership. Case study. INSEAD: The Business School for the World.

32. Arnold, J. A., Arad, S., Rhoades, J. A., & Drasgow, F. (2000). The empowering leadership questionnaire: The construction and validation of a new scale for measuring leader behaviors. Journal of Organizational Behavior, 21 (3), 249-269.

   Conger, J. A. & Kanungo, R. N. (1988). The empowerment process: Integrating theory and practice. Academy of Management Review, 13 (3), 471-482.

33. Hofstede, G., Hofstede, G. J., & Minkov, M. (2010). Cultures and organizations: Software of the mind (3rd ed.). New York, NY: McGraw-Hill.

34. Hofstede Insights (n.d.). Country comparison tool. Retrieved from www.hofstede-insights.com.

Acknowledgements

Pearl

I want to thank my husband, Bobby Thomas for being so patient and supportive during the years it's taken to write this book. I am inspired by your love.

I value the wisdom I acquired through my relationships with clients and colleagues. I appreciate the learnings, encouragement and support.

I'd like to acknowledge my parents – Philomena and Hugh Hilliard – who motivated me and encouraged me to always try my best. Unfortunately, they are no longer with us, but I know they would be very proud. I'm also deeply grateful to my co-author, Denise. She has been such a pleasure to work with – I couldn't have done it without her!

Denise

I'd like to thank my family – my parents (the late Isidro Lopez and my loving mother Estela); my dear siblings Isidro Jr., Francesca and Penelope; my supportive husband Gilbert Santa Maria; and my wonderful sons Miguel and Rafael. Their total belief in me is my source of inspiration.

I'd like to acknowledge my colleagues at Alliant International University, especially Jonathan Troper and Nurcan Ensari, for their support and friendship.

I am grateful to my students, clients and consulting colleagues for whom I am both teacher and learner. And of course, I am thankful to Pearl, my co-author, for taking this challenging writing journey with me. I could not ask for a better writing partner.

Together

Both of us would like to thank Ellen Violette who helped us publish this book. She has a wealth of experience and knowledge as well as a wide network of experts needed in this endeavor. Ellen – your knowledge and wisdom has been invaluable.

Invitation
We have an invitation for you.

We would like to collect more data to assess and improve the psychometric properties of our survey instruments (Appendices A, B and C). We would love to collaborate with you on this endeavor. Or, if you have already administered and collected data using our tools and if you are willing to share your data for validation purposes, please contact us at: info@leadmotivateengage.com. We will maintain the anonymity of all survey participants (and indeed, we will only assess results at the group level, not individual level). We will be happy to share the results of our validation study with you once this is completed.

Please go to https://leadmotivateengage.com/resourcetools/ where you will find the tools and appendices online, in Word format. You can easily customize these forms and checklists to fit your situation.

Thank you so much,

Pearl and Denise

Coaching and Consulting Services

Drs. Pearl Hilliard and Denise Lopez are experienced leadership coaches and consultants, focusing on the following areas:

- Leadership Development
- Employee Engagement
- Team Building
- Strengths Development
- Managing Conflict
- Emotional Intelligence

They undertake coaching, consulting, training and retreat facilitation engagements. They are happy to speak in more depth on the topics addressed in this book. You can find out more information on our website and on LinkedIn -

Website: https://leadmotivateengage.com/
Pearl on LinkedIn: https://www.linkedin.com/in/pearlhilliard/
Denise on LinkedIn: https://www.linkedin.com/in/
patricia-denise-lopez-ph-d-a1b719/

Please contact Pearl and Denise at info@leadmotivateengage.com to discuss your leadership needs.

Biographies

Dr. Pearl Hilliard is the founder of Hilliard Performance Solutions. She brings to clients a wealth of multi-industry experience in strategic organizational development, learning and leadership development, coaching, integrated talent management, organizational improvement and team building. She focuses on performance solutions and results, using appreciative inquiry strategies. Her passion is employee engagement, with an emphasis on a strengths-based approach. She has a successful track record of getting to the root of the issue (in collaboration with the client) and guiding that client to the simplest, most practical solution to achieve their desired results.

Pearl provides leadership, career management and life transitions coaching (both in-person and virtually). She is a Certified Positive Psychology Coach and an Associate Certified Coach. She uses insights from research in the positive psychology field to help her coaching clients overcome barriers, make positive changes in their lives, and achieve breakthrough success.

Pearl received her doctoral degree (Ed.D.) in Human Performance at Work from the University of Southern California.

Dr. Patricia "Denise" Lopez is Professor of Organizational Psychology at Alliant International University where she teaches and conducts research in leadership, work motivation and productivity, team effectiveness, and organizational change management. Denise considers it her mission to develop great leaders and build workplaces to which people can bring their best and most enthusiastic selves. Over the last 25 years, she has taught, trained, coached and consulted with diverse managers, teams and organizations in the United States and Asia-Pacific.

Denise received her doctorate (PhD) in Organizational Psychology from Columbia University Teachers College and has a coaching credential from the International Coaching Federation. She is a founding partner of Global Thought Partners, an organizational consulting and advisory firm. As an organizational consultant, she is known for her strategic perspective, analytic thinking, and ability to facilitate engaging and productive sessions that bring together diverse groups of employees. As a leadership coach and trainer, her unique strength is her ability to deliver engaging discussions and design creative learning opportunities that expand managerial thinking, deepen personal awareness and growth, and identify concrete opportunities and solutions for personal and organizational success.

Printed in Great Britain
by Amazon

44927404R00225